ANCIENT EGYPTIAN
READINGS

WIM VAN DEN DUNGEN

ANCIENT EGYPTIAN

READINGS

Originally published in 2011 by Wim van den Dungen as *Ancient Egyptian Wisdom Readings* at : *www.maat.sofiatopia.org*

© 2016 Wim van den Dungen

All Rights Reserved. Except for brief quotations in a review, this book, or parts thereof, must not be reproduced in any form whatsoever without permission from the publisher.

First edition in 2011 by *www.sofiatopia.org*
Second revised edition in 2016 by Taurus Press

POD Publication
Published for Taurus Press
by LULU.com

ISBN : 978-1-329-65649-9
BISAC : Literary Collections / Ancient, Classical and Medieval

Press

TAURUS Press
Brasschaat - Belgium

Printed on FSC (Forest Stewardship Council) certified paper. This means the acid-free, lead-free, buffered paper of this book is made from wood-based pulp. It also meets the ISO 9706 standard for permanent paper. The vision of the FSC is an economically prosperous management of the world's forests, securing their health for future generations.

no one is born wise
Ptahhotep

Contents

Preface	ix
Introduction	1
Instruction of Hordedef	7
Instruction to Kagemni	9
Maxims of Ptahhotep	13
Pyramid Texts of Unas	34
Instruction to Merikare	149
To Become Magic	161
Discourse of a Man with his Ba	163
Instruction of Amenemhat	171
Great Hymn to the Aten	177
Hymns to Amun	184
The Shabaka Stone	195
Instruction of Amen-em-apt	203
The Adoration of Re	222
Notes	225
Bibliography	233

Preface

In 1983, studying Middle Egyptian in the Department of Oriental Philology at Ghent University, professor Herman De Meulenaere tried to inculcate on us students the value of drawing our hieroglyphs elegantly.

As a student of philosophy, my main interest lay in the language and its literature. Moreover, unable to draw, I quickly moved to transliterations. Had my teacher, with a deep sigh, not told me my version of the letter 'f' (so crucial in grammar), and representing a horned viper (*Cerastes cornulus*), looked like a small worm ? Likewise with the birds, with eagles looking like chickens ...

Years later, discovering the roots of monotheism in the many teachings of Ancient Kemet, I was prompted to again invest time and effort to grasp what these thinkers of old had contributed to Mediterranean sapience, religion and spirituality and well beyond.

So if I wanted to try to come to understand the Ancient Egyptian mentality beyond what others had taught me and had published about it, I had to constitute and translate my own choice of Egyptian texts. Besides, recent linguistic advances in understanding the verbal form (Loprieno, 1995), combined with novel insights into the evanescent concept of 'god' ('nTr', 'netjer' – Hornung, 1971), prompt a revision of most important texts. As the Egyptians were never silent about the gods, a relevant choice had to be made.

In 2001, I embarked upon a translation project of which this book is the end result. It contains English translations of thirteen major texts, including the complete *Pyramid Texts* of Unas, as well as a French translation of a selection of hymns from the remarkable *Hymns to Amun*.

In 2006, Buddhism and the 'dharmic' approach gave rise to *www.bodhi.sofiatopia.org*.

It took me nine years to be able to start comparing the Vajrayāna and its shamanism (cf. Indian Shaivism, Tibetan *Bön*) with Ancient Egyptian (temple) shamanism. This exercise in cross-cultural correspondence would not have been possible without the translations offered here.

These texts constitute the textual backbone of my investigations into Ancient Egyptian sapience, magic, theology, ritual and ceremonialism, to be complemented by *The Twelve Hours of the Night*, a forthcoming study of the *Amduat*.

Of all egyptologists I had the privilege to learn from, I particularly wish to thank Herman De Meulenaere.

The various publications of Alexandre Piankoff, James Henry Breasted, Wallis Budge, Kurt Sethe, Henri Frankfort, Alan Gardiner, Erik Hornung, Jan Assmann, Raymond Faulkner, Miriam Lichtheim, James Allen, Serge Sauneron, Christian Jacq, and Jeremy Naydler were of particular interest to me. And yes, de Lubicz too.

I wish to thank Theodore Abt for his depth psychological analysis of the *Amduat*. Did Carl Gustav Jung, in order to identify the visible marks of the archetypes of the collective unconscious, not study astrology, magic and alchemy ?

Finally, a special thanks to those scholars of the Egyptian language who's excellent translations have assisted my more literal take, in particular Budge, Breasted, Piankoff, Lichtheim, Faulkner and Allen.

I wish these translations to assist our understanding of the grand Ancient Egyptian civilization ; contributing to a readable introduction to its sacred literature.

Wim van den Dungen
January 2016
Brasschaat

Introduction

This book offers a choice of translations of Egyptian texts in English (and one in French), bringing to life the sapience, ritual, magic and theology at work in the 'House of Life' that was Egypt. This gives rise to three registers : sapiential, ceremonial and magico-theological.

The first register includes :

Instruction of Hordedef
Instruction to Kagemni
Maxims of Ptahhotep
Instruction to Merikare
Instruction of Amenemhat
Instruction of Amen-em-apt

The ceremonial register contains an integral translation of the oldest corpus of religious texts in the world, the *Pyramid Texts* of Unas, the last king of the Vth Dynasty, interred about 2348 BCE.

The *Pyramid Texts* entertain a rhythmicization of their teachings, have dramatic structures at work and make use of repetitions. These refer to the dramatic, initiatic, and performative intent imbedded in this remarkable *corpus* of texts, containing funerary and *this-life* rituals.

The magico-theological register pertains to the power of magic, the goal of life, death and the afterlife, natural religion, henotheistic theology, and peeks into the philosophy of mind of the Ancient Egyptians.

To Become Magic
The Discourse of a Man with his Ba
The Great Hymn to the Aten
Hymns to Amun (with French translation)
The Shabaka Stone
The Adoration of Re

These readings span a period of 13 centuries, covering most periods of Pharaonic Egypt : the Old Kingdom (ca. 2670 – 2205 BCE), the First Intermediate Period (ca. 2198 – 1938 BCE), the Middle Kingdom (ca. 1938 – 1759 BCE), and the New Kingdom (ca. 1539 – 1075 BCE).

The development of Egyptian literature, from solitary hieroglyphs (in the Predynastic Period) to its classical form (in the Middle Kingdom) keeps pace with the characteristics of the first stages of our cognitive genesis, the so-called 'ante-rational stage' of cognition. These early stages are mythical, imaginal, concrete and bound to a concrete, given context (abductive instead of deductive or inductive).

An understanding of these features helps to discover the linguistic layeredness or palimpsestic stratification present in a text, calling us to investigate its general, medial and immediate contexts, as were it an archeological object of its own. It is interesting to translate Egyptian texts with this 'filter' in mind. In the ante-rational mind of children worldwide, Piaget and genetic epistemology discovered three logics at work. These strata are different and interacting :

• mythical logic : notions are developed without clear distinction between the source of thought, the mind, and its clustering, constellational stream of thoughts.

Events are put together on the basis of a shared concrete meaning, explicit or not, in terms of physical processes, like any rhythmical or recurring pattern (coordination of actions) or signal ;

• pre-rational logic : the formation of pre-concepts and a more stable source of thought or primitive subjectivity, one still linked to the coordination of actions (and not yet, to a concrete conceptual model). Psychomorph, active iconization happens and grammatical structures are worked out. Contradictions are not reconciled. Concepts have no stability outside their ritual or practical use and are always linked to person(s), place and time.

• proto-rational logic : based on a real conceptual structure having practical (not theoretical) tools to manipulate thoughts. In order to solve problems abductively, subject and object are distinguished and mental operations have 'closure'. This never leads to any discursive articulation (and its conceptual freedom), because of the ever-present context to which the concrete operations remain bound.

Ancient Egyptian civilization as a whole never attained the next stages of cognitive growth : the formal, critical, creative and nondual modes of cognition. The first two encompass rationality (apprehension, conceptual reason), the last two meta-rationality (prehension, intuition). These stages, and the epistemology to which they give rise, can be found in *The Book of Lemmas* (2014), available at : www.sofiatopia.org/equiaeon/lemmas.htm.

Kemet never escaped context. In their theologies (of Atum-Re, Ptah, Thoth, Osiris and Thebes), this works out as a 'constellational view' on the deities, always appearing as 'families'. The libidinal (mythical), tribal (pre-rationality) and imitative (proto-rationality) styles intermingle and form a *multi-layered reality* in which the dualities are transcended by the divine king and his representatives.

Because Ancient Egyptian civilization never relinquished a contextual (abductive) approach, no formal, abstract framework was ever put in place. To reflect this, words like 'divine', 'god', 'goddess' and 'pantheon' are not capitalized.

Only in the *Great Hymn to the Aten*, the *Hymns to Amun* and the *Adoration of Re* is this restriction lifted, for these exceptional texts evidence the way an exceptional individual (like Akhenaten), or a group of such individuals (like some Heliopolitans or the late New Kingdom Theban priesthood) did at times embrace some *formal notion* of the Divine, either in terms of a proto-monotheism (of the Aten), or as the henotheism of Re or Amun. When this happens 'God' and 'Gods' are accepted formats, but this happens only a few times.

ante-rationality	in Egyptian literature	in Middle Egyptian
mythical	Gerzean ware design schemata early palettes	individual hieroglyps no texts no grammar, 'cartoon' style
pre-rational	Reliefs Biographies Inscriptions Testamentary Enactments Pyramid Texts	words in archaic sentences in 'record' style rudimentary grammar
proto-rational	Maxims of Ptahhotep, Coffin Texts, Sapiental literature Great Hymn to the Aten Memphis Theology, etc.	from simple sentences to a classical literary language capable of further change as well as interiorization

Because of its anterational features, Egyptian favors a *multiplicity of approaches* (Frankfort), accommodating a wide range of possible translations. Here, a rather literal methodology was adopted. No doubt a poetical and free mode would bring other semantic layers to the surface.

Translations are in chronological order. Titles in capitals were added to assist reading. These codes clarifly the text :

(...) : textual additions to bring out the sense and/or to clarify ;
<...> : conjectured translation of unknown word or a brief documentary remark ;
[...] : fragmentary, uncertain or corrupt word or passage, but restored ;
[...] : uncertain or corrupt word or passage ;
--- : short lacuna ;
------ : long lacunae or a section of text with a lot of lacunae ;
... : incomprehensible word or passage.

the Scribe of Saqqara
IVth or Vth Dynasty
Louvre

The Old Kingdom

The Instruction of Hordedef

son of Pharaoh Khufu - reconstructed fragment – Vth Dynasty – Old Kingdom – ca.2400 BCE [1]

PROLOGUE

Beginning of the written teaching made by the hereditary prince, count, King's son, Hordedef, for his son, his nursling, whose name is Au-Ib-Re.

THE TEACHING

He says :

'Cleanse yourself before your own eyes, lest another cleanse You.

When You prosper, found your household, take a mistress of heart, a son will be born to You.

It is for the son that You build a house when You make a place for yourself.

Make a good dwelling in the graveyard, make worthy your station in the West.

Accept death humbles us, accept life exalts us, the house of death is for life. Seek for yourself well-watered fields.

Choose for him (the funerary priest) a plot among your fields, well-watered every year.

He profits You more than your own son, prefer him even to your --- '

Munich Ostracon 3400

The Instruction to Kagemni

vizier of Pharaoh Snefru – fragment – VIth Dynasty – late Old Kingdom – ca.2200 BCE [2]

' --- the timid man prospers,
praised is the fitting,
open (is) the tent to the silent,
spacious is the seat of the satisfied.

Speak not ! Sharp are the knives against he who transgresses the road, (he is) without speedy advance, except when he faults.

When You sit with company,
shun the food You like.
Restraint of heart is (only) a brief moment !
Gluttony is base and one points the finger at it.

A cup of water quenches thirst,
a mouthful of herbs strengthens the heart.

A single good thing
stands for goodness as a whole,
a little something stands for much.

Vile is he whose belly is voracious ;
time passes and he forgets
in whose house the belly strides.

When You sit with a glutton,
eat when his appetite has passed.
When You drink with a drunkard,
partake when his heart is happy.

Do not grab (your) meat
by the side of a glutton,
(but) take when he gives You,
do not refuse it, then it will soothe.

He who is blameless in matters of food,
no word can prevail against him.

The shy of face, even impassive of heart,
the harsh is kinder to him than to his (own) mother, all people are his servants.

Let your name go forth,
while You are silent with your mouth.
When You are summoned,
be not great of heart, because of your strength among those your age, lest You be opposed.

One knows not what may happen, and what god does when he punishes.

The vizier had his children summoned, after he had gained a complete knowledge of the ways of men, their character having come upon him.

In the end he said to them :

"All that is written in this book, heed it as I said it. Do not go beyond what has been set down."

Then they placed themselves on their bellies. They recited it aloud as it was written. It was good in their hearts beyond anything in this entire land. They stood and sat accordingly.

Then the Majesty of King Huni of Upper and Lower Egypt died.

The Majesty of King Snefru of Upper and Lower Egypt was raised up as beneficient King in this entire land.

Kagemni was (then) made overseer of the city and vizier.'

It is finished.

Restraint of heart
is (only) a brief moment !

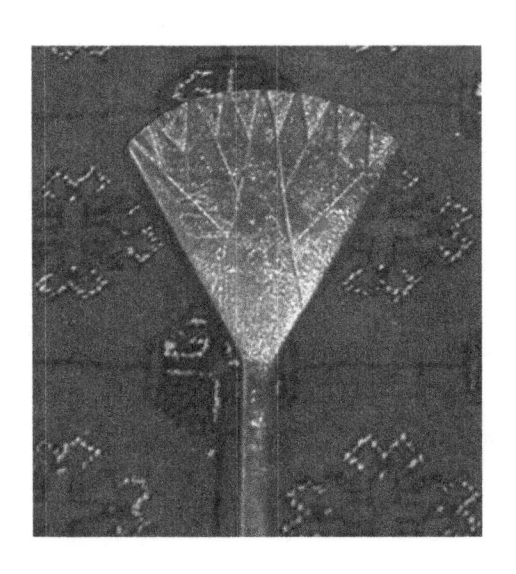

Upper half of the Lotus Staff
after an XVIIIth Dynasty model

The Maxims of Good Discourse

by vizier Ptahhotep – complete – VIth Dynasty – late Old Kingdom – ca.2200 BCE [3]

PROLOGUE

Written teachings of the overseer of the city, the vizier Ptahhotep, under the Majesty of Pharaoh Izezi, King of Upper and Lower Egypt, may he live for ever and ever !

The overseer of the city,
the vizier Ptahhotep, he says :

'Sovereign, my Lord !
Old age is here, old age arrives !
Exhaustion comes, weakness is made new.
One lies down in discomfort all day,
eyes are dim, ears deaf,
strength wanes, the heart is weary.
The mouth, silent, speaks not,
the heart, ended, recalls not the past,
the bones ache throughout.
Good becomes evil,
all taste is gone.
What age does to people
is evil in everything.

The nose clogged, breathes not,
difficult are standing and sitting.

May this servant be commanded
to make a "Staff of Old Age"!
so as to speak to him the words of the judges,
the ways of those before,
who listened to the gods.

May the like be done for You,
so that strife may be removed from the people,
and the Two Shores may serve You.'

The majesty of this god said:

'As for You, teach him then the sayings of the past, so that he may become a good example for the children of the great. May hearing enter him and the exactness of every heart that speaks to him.

No one is born wise.'

THE TEACHING

Beginning of the maxims of good discourse, spoken by the prince, count, god's father, beloved of god, eldest son of the King, of his body, overseer of the city, vizier Ptahhotep, teaching the ignorant in knowledge, and in the standard of good discourse, beneficial to him who hears, but woe to him who neglects them.

So he spoke to his son:

'Don't let your heart get big
because of your knowledge.
Take counsel with the ignorant
as well as with the scholar.
(For) the limits of art are not brought,
(and) no artisan is equipped with perfection.
Good discourse is more hidden than green stone, yet may be found among the maids at the grindstones.

2

If You meet a disputant in his moment, one who directs his heart, superior to You, fold your arms and bend your back. Do not seize your heart against him, (for) he will never agree with You.

Belittle the evil speech, by not opposing him while he is in his moment. He will be called a know-nothing when your control of heart will match his piles (of words).

3

If You meet a disputant in his moment (of action) who is your equal, your peer, You will make your excellence exceed his by silence, (even) while he is speaking wrongly.

There will be much talk among the hearers, (and) the knowledge the magistrates have of your name will be good.

4

If You meet a disputant in his moment, a man of little, not at all your equal, do not be aggressive of heart because he is weak, give him land (for) he will refute himself.

Do not answer him to relieve your heart. Do not wash the heart against your opponent. Wretched is he who injures a man of little heart. One will wish to do what your heart desires. You will strike him with the reproof of the magistrates.

5

If You are a man who leads, charged to direct the affairs of a great number, seek out every well adjusted deed, so that your conduct may be blameless.

Great is Ma'at, lasting in effect.
Undisturbed since the time of Osiris.
One punishes the transgressor of laws,
though the heart that robs overlooks this.

Baseness may seize riches,
yet crime never lands its wares.
He says : "I acquire for myself."
He does not say : "I acquire for my function."

In the end, it is Ma'at that lasts,
(and) man says :
"It is my father's domain."

6

Do not scheme against people,
(for) god punishes accordingly.
If a man (nevertheless) says :
"I shall live that way."
he will lack bread for his mouth.

If a man says : "I shall be rich."
He will have to say :

"My cleverness has snared me."
If a man says : "I will rob someone."
he will, in the end, make a gift to a stranger !
People's schemes do not prevail.
God's command is what prevails.

Live then in the midst of peace (with what You have),
(for) what they (the gods) give comes by itself.

7

If You get to be among guests,
at the dining table of one greater than You,
accept what he gives,
in the way it is set before your nose.

Look at what is before You,
do not pierce it with lots of glances :
it offends the Ka to be molested.
Do not speak until he summons,
(since) one does not know
whether he has evil on his heart.
Speak when he addresses You,
and may your words please the heart.
The nobleman, sitting behind the breads,
behaves as his Ka commands him.
He will give to him whom he favors,
(for) that is the custom
when the night has come.

It is the Ka that makes his hands reach out.
The great man gives to the lucky man.

Thus the breads are eaten
under the plan of god,
a fool is who complains of it.

8

If You are a man of trust,
sent by one great man to another,
be exact when he sends You.

Give his message as he said it.
Guard against slanderous speech,
which embroils one great with another.

Keep to Ma'at, do not exceed it.

But the washing of the heart
should not be repeated.

Do not speak against anyone,
great or small, the Ka abhors it.

9

If You plow and there is growth in the field, (because) god lets it prosper in your hand, do not boast about it at your neighbour's side, for one has great respect for the silent man.

If a man of good character is a man of wealth, he takes possession like a crocodile, even in court.

Do not impose on one who is childless,
neither criticize, nor boast of it.

There is many a father who has grief, and a mother of children less content than another (without).

It is the lonely whom god fosters,
while the family man prays for a follower.

10

If You are a weakling, serve a man of quality, worthy of trust, (so) that all your conduct may be well with god. Do not recall if once he was of humble condition, do not let your heart become big toward him, for knowing his former state.

Respect him for what has accrued to him, for surely goods do not come by themselves. They are their laws for him whom they (the gods) love.

His gain, he gathered it himself, (but) it is god who makes him worthy, and protects him while he sleeps.

11

Follow your heart as long as You live.
Do no more than is required.
Do not shorten the time of "follow-the-heart", (for) trimming its moment offends the Ka.

Do not waste time on daily cares
beyond providing for your household.
When wealth has come, follow your heart !
Wealth does no good if one is annoyed !

12

If You are a man of quality, worthy of trust, may You produce a son, by the favour of god. If he is straight, turns around your character, takes care of your possessions in good order, (then) accomplish for him all that is good. He is your son, belonging to the seed of your Ka, (so) do not withdraw your heart from him.

But an offspring can make trouble :
if he goes into the wrong direction,
neglects your counsel,
with insolence disobeys all that is said,
if his mouth sprouts evil speech,
(then) put him to work
for the totality of his talk !
They disfavour him who crosses You,
(for) his obstacle was fated in the womb.
He whom they guide can not go astray,
(but) whom they make boatless can not cross.

13

If You are in a court of justice,
stand or sit as fits your rank,
assigned to You on the first day.
Do not force your way in,
(for) You will be turned back.
Keen is the face of him who enters announced,
spacious the seat of him who has been called.

The court of justice has a correct method,
all behavior is by the plumb-line.
It is god who gives the seat.
He who uses elbows is not helped.

14

If You are among the people,
gain allies through being trustful of heart.

The trustful of heart
does not vent his belly's speech.
He will himself become a man who commands,
a man of means thanks to his behavior.

May your name be good
without You talking about it.
Your body is sleek, your face turns towards your
people, and one praises You
without You knowing (it).
(But) him whose heart obeys his belly disappears ; he
raises contempt of himself in place of love. His heart is
denuded, his body unanointed.

The great of heart is a gift of god.
He who obeys his belly, obeys the enemy.

15

Report your commission
without swallowing the heart,
and give your advise in your master's council.

If he is fluent in his speech,
it will not be hard for the envoy to report,
nor will he be answered :
"Who is he to know it ?"

As to the master, his affairs will fail,
if he plans to punish him for it.

He should be silent and conclude :
"I have spoken."

16

If You are a man who leads,
that your way to govern may freely travel.

You should do outstanding things.
Remember the day that comes after,
(so that) no strife will occur
in the midst of honors.

(Indeed), where a hiding crocodile emerges,
hatred arises.

17

If You are a man who leads,
calmly hear the speech of one who pleads,
(and) do not stop him from purging his body
of that which he planned to tell.
A man in distress wants to wash his heart
more than that his case be won.
About him who stops a plea,
one says : "Why does he reject it ?"
Not all one pleads for can be granted,
but a good hearing calms the heart.

18

If You want friendship to endure
in the house You enter,
as master, brother, or friend,
or in whatever place You enter,
beware of approaching the women !
Unhappy is the place where it is done.
(Their) face is not keen on he who intrudes on them.
A thousand men are turned away from their good.
A short moment like a dream, then death comes for
having known them.

Poor advice is "shoot the opponent"!
When one goes to do it, the heart rejects it.

(But) as for him who fails through lust of them,
no affair of his can prosper.

19

If You want your conduct to be perfect,
deliver yourself from every evil,
(and) combat against the greed of the heart.
It is a grievous sickness without cure,
impossible to penetrate.
It causes disaster among fathers and mothers,
among the brothers of the mother,
and parts wife from husband.
It is an amalgam of all evils,
a bundle of all hateful things.

That man endures who correctly applies Ma'at,
and walks according to his stride.
He will make a will by it.

The greedy of heart has no tomb!

20

Do not be greedy of heart
in the division (of goods).

Do not covet more than your share.
Do not be greedy of heart toward your kin.

The kind has a greater claim than the rude.
The family of the latter reveals very little,
(for) he is deprived of what speech brings.
Even a little of what is craved, makes conflict rise in a cool-bellied man.

21

When You prosper, found your house,
love your wife with ardor,
fill her belly, clothe her back,
ointment is a remedy for her body.
Gladden her heart as long as You live.
She is a fertile field, useful to her master.
Do not contend with her in a court of justice,
(and) keep her from power, restrain her.
Her eye is her storm when she gazes.
You will make her stay in your house.
If You push her back, see the tears !
Her vagina is one of her forms of action.
What she enforces,
is that a canal be made for her.

22

Satisfy those who enter, and in whom You trust,
with what You make,
(for) You make it by the favour of god.
Of him who fails to satisfy those who enter,
and in whom he trusts, one says :
"A Ka too pleased with itself !".
What will come is unknown,
even if one understands tomorrow.
The (proper) Ka is a correct Ka
at peace with itself.
If praiseworthy deeds are done,
trustworthy friends will say : "Welcome !"

One does not bring supplies to town,
one brings friends when there is need.

23

Do not repeat calumny, neither hear it.
It is the way of expression of the hot-bellied.
Report a thing observed, not heard.

If it is negligible, do not say anything,
(and) see : he who is before You recognizes (your) worth.

Let it be ordered to seize what it produces.
In accordance with the law, hatred will arise against him who seizes it to use it. Calumny is like a vision against which one covers the face.

24

If You are a man of quality, worthy of trust,
who sits in his master's council, bring your whole heart together towards excellence.

Your silence is more useful than chatter.
Speak when You know how to untie the knot.
It is the skilled who speak in council.

Speaking is harder than all other work.
He who unties it makes it serve.

25

If You are mighty, gain respect through knowledge and gentleness of speech.

Do not command except as is fitting.
He who provokes gets into trouble.
Do not be high of heart, lest You be humbled.

Do not be mute, lest You be reprimanded.
When You answer one who is fuming,
avert your face, control yourself,
(for) the flames of the hot of heart sweep across.
He who steps gently finds his path paved.

All day long the sad of heart has no happy moment.
All day long the frivolous of heart can not keep house.

The archers complete the aim, as one who holds the
rudder untill (it) touches land.

The opposant is imprisoned.
He who obeys his heart is equipped to order.

26

Do not oppose a great man's action.
Do not vex the heart of one who is burdened.
His anger manifests against him who combats him.
The Ka will part from him who loves him.

(Yet) he who provides is together with god.
What he wishes will be done for him.
When he turns his face back to You after raging, (then)
there will be peace from his Ka,
(and) hostility from the enemy.

To provide increases love.

27

Teach the great what is useful to him,
be his aid before the people.

Let his knowledge fall back on his master,
(and) your sustenance will come from his Ka.

As the favorite's belly is filled,
so your back is clothed by it,
and his help will be there to sustain You.

For your superior whom You love, and who lives by it,
he in turn will give You good support. Thus will love of
You endure, in the belly of those who love You.

Behold :
it is the Ka that loves to listen.

If You are a magistrate of standing,
commissioned to appease the many,
remove stupidity from the record.

When You speak, do not lean to one side,
beware lest one complain :
"Judges, he puts his speech
on the side he likes !"

In court, your deeds
will (then) turn against You.

29

If You are angered by a misdeed,
(then) lean toward the man (only)
on account of his rectitude.

Pass over the old error, do not recall it,
since he was silent to You on the first day.

30

If You are great after having been humble,
have gained wealth after having been poor in the past,
in a town which You know,
(then) knowing your former condition,
do not put the trust of your heart in your heaps,
which came to You as gifts of god,
so that You will not fall behind one like You,
to whom the same has happened.

31

Bend your back to your superior,
your overseer from the palace,
then your house will endure in its wealth,
and your rewards (will be) in their right place.

Wretched is he who opposes a superior,
(for) one lives as long as he is mild ...
Baring the arm does not hurt it !

Do not plunder a neighbour's house,
(and) do not steal the goods of one near You,
so that he does not denounce You,
before You are heard.

A quarreler lacks in heart, so if he is known as an aggressor, the hostile will have trouble in the neighbourhood.

32

Do not copulate with a woman-boy,
for You know that one will fight
against the water upon her heart.

What is in her belly will not be refreshed.
That during the night she does not do what is repelled,
(but) be calmed after having ended
the offence of her heart.

33

If You seek to probe the true nature of a friend, do not inquire (after him), but approach him (yourself).

(Then) deal with him alone,
until You are no longer uncertain about his condition.

After a time, dispute with him.
Test his heart in dialogue.
If what he has seen (of himself) escapes him,
if he does a thing that irritates You,
be yet friendly with him or be silent,
but do not turn away your face.
Restrain yourself and open dialogue.
Do not answer with an act of hostility.

Neither counter him, nor humiliate him.
His time does not fail to come ...
One does not escape what is fated.

34

Be bright-faced as long as You exist !
(But) what leaves the storehouse does not return.
It is the food to be distributed which is coveted.

(But) one whose belly is empty is an accuser,
(and) one deprived becomes an opponent.
Do not have him for a neighbour.

Kindness is a man's memorial
for the years after the function.

35

Know those at your side,
then your goods endure.
Do not be weak of character toward your friends,
(they are) a riverbank to be turned and filled,
more important than its riches ...
For what belongs to one
(also) belongs to another !
The good deed profits the son-of-man.
An accomplished nature is a memorial.

36

Punish as a commander-in-chief,
(but) teach the complete form !
The act of stopping crime
is an enduring good example.

Crime, except for misfortune,
turns the complainer into an aggressor.

37

If You take to wife a woman of good quality, who is unbound of heart and known by her town, conform her to the double law. Be pleasant to her when the moment is right, do not separate yourself from her and let her eat. The joyful of heart confer an exact balance.

THE EPILOGUE

on hearing and listening

If You hear my sayings,
all your plans will go forward.
In their act of Ma'at lies their value.
Their memory lingers on in the speech of men,
because of the accomplishment of their command !
If every word is carried on,
they will not perish in this land.

That an advice be given for the good,
(so that) the great will speak accordingly.
It is teaching a man to speak
to what comes after (him).
He who hears this becomes a master-hearer.
It is good to speak to posterity, it will hear it.
If a good example is set by him who leads,
he will be beneficient for ever,
(and) his wisdom will be for all time.
He who knows, feeds his Ba with what endures,
so that it is happy with him on earth.
He who knows is known by his wisdom,
(and) the great by his good actions.
(That) his heart twines his tongue,
(and) his lips (be) precise when he speaks.
That his eyes see !
That his ears be pleased
to hear what profits his son.

(For) acting with Ma'at,
he is free of falsehood.

Useful is listening to a son who hears !
If hearing enters the hearer,
the hearer becomes a listener.
To listen well is to speak well.
He who listens is a master of what is good.
Splendid is listening to one who hears !
Listening is better than all else.
It manifests perfect love.

How good it is for a son
to grasp his father's words !
Underneath them, he will reach old age.

on the listener and the non-listener

He who listens is beloved of god,
he who does not listen is hated by god.
(It is) the heart (which) makes of its owner
a listener or a non-listener.

Life, prosperity and health are a man's heart.
Its the hearer who listens to what is said.

He who loves to listen,
is one who does what is said.
How good for a son to obey his father !

How happy is he (the son) to whom it is said :
"The son pleases as a master of listening."
He (the son) who hears the one (the father) who said
this, is well adjusted in his inner being,
and honored by his father.
His remembrance is in the mouth of the living,
those on earth and those who will be.
If the son-of-man accepts his father's words,
no plan of his will go wrong.
Teach your son to be a hearer,

one who will be valued by the heart of the nobles,
one who guides his mouth by what he was told,
one regarded as a listener.
This son excels, his deeds stand out,
while failure enters him who listens not.

The knower wakes early to his lasting form,
while the fool is hard pressed.

The fool who does not listen,
can accomplish nothing at all.
He sees knowledge as ignorance,
usefulness as harmfulness.
He does all that is detestable,
and is blamed for it each day.
He lives on that by which one dies,
he feeds on damned speech.
His sort is known to the officials,
to wit : "A living death each day !"
One passes over his doings,
because of his many daily troubles.

A son who listens, is a "Follower of Horus".
It goes well with him when he listens.
When he is old and reaches veneration,
(may) he speak likewise to his children,
renewing the teaching of his father.
Every man teaches as he acts.
May he speak to the children,
so that they may speak to their children.
Set an example, do not give offense.
If Ma'at stands firm, your children live !

As to the first who comes as a carrier of evil,
may people say to what they see :
"That is then just like him !"
And may they say to what they hear :
"That is then just like him !"

Let everyone see them (the children)
to appease the multitudes.
Without them, riches are useless.

on speaking

Do not take a word and then bring it back.
Do not put one thing in place of another.
Beware of loosening the cords in You,
lest a man of knowledge say : "Hear ! If You want to endure in the mouth of the listeners, speak (only) after You have mastered the craft !"

If You speak in a refined way,
all your plans will be in place.
Immerge your heart, control your mouth,
then You are known among the officials.

Be quite exact before your master,
act so that he says : "He is a son !"

And those who hear it will say :
"Blessed is he to whom he was born !"

Be patient of heart the moment You speak,
so as to say elevated things.
In this way, the nobles who hear it will say :
"How good is what comes from his mouth !"

Act so that your master will say of You : "How accomplished is he whom his father taught. When he came forth from him, issued from his body, he (the father) spoke to him when he was in the belly (of his mother), and he (the son) accomplished even more than he was told." Lo, the good son, the gift of god, exceeds what is told to him by his master, he does Ma'at and his heart matches his steps.

(O my son) as You succeed me, with a sound body, the King at peace with all what is done, may You obtain many years of life !'

concluding remarks

Not small is what I did on earth ...
I had hundred and ten years of life,
as a gift of the King, (and)
honors exceeding those of the ancestors.
For by doing Ma'at for the King,
the venerated place comes.

colophon

From its beginning to its end, in accordance with (how it was) found in writing.

The knower wakes early to his lasting form,
while the fool is hard pressed.

The Pyramid Texts of King Unas

as found in his tomb – complete – Vth Dynasty – late Old Kingdom – ca.2350 BCE [4]

King Unas (ca. 2378 – 2348 BCE), was the first to include hieroglyphic inscriptions in the corridor, antechamber, passage-way and burial chamber of his tomb. This coincides with an increase of writing in the late Vth Dynasty (ca. 2487 – 2348 BCE), as well as new insights in the magical power of words (besides grave goods). The area around the royal sarcophagus as well as the *serdab* or 'Ka' chamber are uninscribed.

The *Pyramid Texts* of Unas, carved in Tura limestone and filled with blue pigment, contain, in over two hundred 'spells', the first historical account of the (Heliopolitan) religion of the Old Kingdom, in particular its *royal cult*. The texts of Unas became canonical. They precede the textualization of the *Vedas* (ca. 1900 BCE). Discovered by Maspero in 1881, these texts had been buried and left *undisturbed* for ca. 4200 years ; an *uncorrupted* primary religious source !

These texts are a *corpus* of 'utterances' or 'spells', so called because most sayings begin with the expression 'Dd mdw' ('Dd' = 'word' ; 'mdw' = 'speech'), 'to say' or 'to say the words', i.e. sacred words to be recited. In the translation, each spell is numbered. The first number refers to the ordinal position of the spell in the present English version (of 232 sayings), while the second is the enumeration of the text by Sethe (1908).

Together with the spells found in the tombs of Teti, Pepi I, Merenre, Pepi II and his wives Neith, Ipwet and Oudjebeten of the VIth Dynasty and King Iby of the VIIIth Dynasty, they constitute the *Pyramid Texts*.

That ritual actions took place during the recitation of protective spells and offerings, can be inferred by the presence of instructions like 'to say the words four times', 'pour libation', 'burn incense', etc. or by the description of the offering at hand. These dramatical instructions have been *italicized* and integrated precisely where this was the case in the original. As remnants of the original papyrus copies can be detected, we may conjecture some spells also refer to *this-life* rituals.

The royal cartouche with the name 'Wenis', 'Unas' or 'Unis' is translated as 'King Unas' each time an original first-person context is not given. When Unas speaks, the cartouche is translated as 'I, King Unas' when appearing for the first time and 'I' or 'me' in all other instances of the same utterance. The king's speech is preceded by 'by the king', the priest's speech by 'by the priest'. When other gods or sacred objects speak, this is given in the original text and translated.

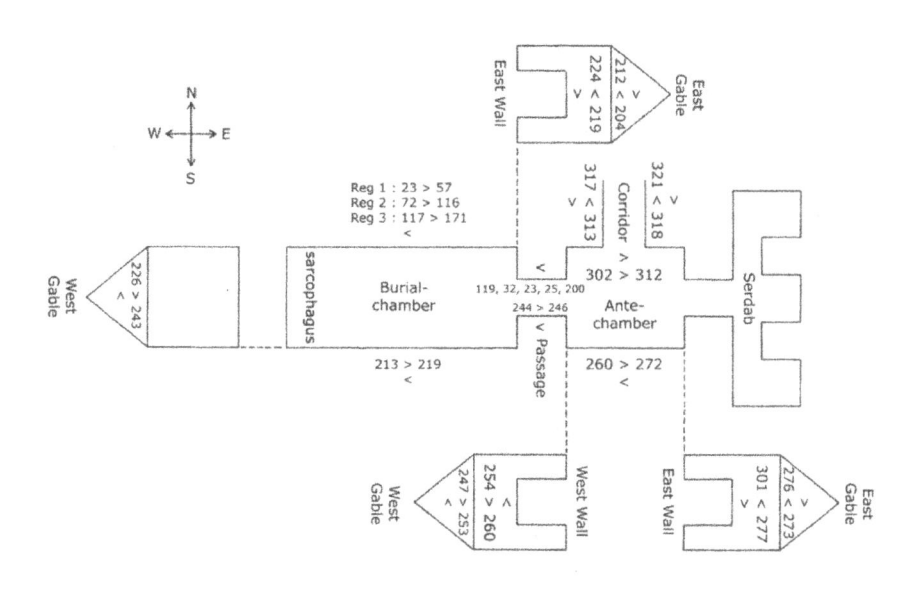

the tomb of king Unas
with Sethe-number and direction of the hieroglyphs

The Burial Chamber
The Land of Osiris

Protection of the Sarcophagus
West Gable

all by the priest, except 5 and 15

1 (226)

To say the words :

'Entwined is a Plait-snake
by another Plait-snake,
(and this) toothless calf which came forth from the
pasture has been entwined.
Earth, swallow up
what has emerged from You !

Monster, lie down !
Crawl away !

The Majesty of the Pelican
has fallen in the water.
Snake, turn over,
that Re may see You !'

2 (227)

To say the words :

'The head of the Great Black Bull
has been cut off.
Hepenu-snake, I say this against You !
God-repelling scorpion, I say this against You !
Turn over, slide into the Earth,
for I have said this against You.'

3 (228)

To say the words :

'One face has fallen on another face !
One face has seen another face !
The coloured knife, black and green,
has gone against it.
It has swallowed the one it has licked.'

4 (229)

To say the words :

'This here is the fingernail of Atum, pressed on the knot of the vertebrae of Nehebu-Kas (the serpent deity), the one which stilled the turmoil from Hermopolis.

Fall down !
Crawl away !'

5 (230)

The two spells of Elephantine.

by the priest :

To say the words :

'Your two <poison-fangs> into the Earth !
Your two ribs into the hole !

Shoot liquid while the Two Kites will stand up. Your mouth will be closed by the instrument of punishment, and the mouth of the instrument of punishment will be closed by Mafdet. The made <weary> will be bitten by the plait serpent.'

by the King :

'O Re, I, King Unas, have bitten the Earth.
I have bitten Geb.
I have bitten the father
of him who would bite me.

This one is the one who would bite me, I did not bite him. He bit me at the instant after seeing me. It was he who came against me, I did not go against him.

If You bite me, I will cause You to be alone ;
(but) if You (only) look at me,
I will permit You to have your companion.'

by the priest :

'The plait serpent has been bitten by a serpent, a serpent has been bitten by the plait serpent. The sky will entwine, the Earth will entwine. The male who turns around the people will entwine, the god Blind-is-his-head will entwine, and You yourself, scorpion, will be entwined.

These are the two spells of Elephantine which are in the mouth of Osiris, which Horus has cast on the backbone (of the snake).'

6 (231)

To say the words :

'Your bone is a harpoon and You are harpooned. The hostile hearts are <held off>, and the pillars who are in the kiln's place are felled. That is Hemen !'

7 (232)

To say the words :

'Vascular one, vascular one !
Seminal one, seminal one !

You long one of his mother,
You long one of his mother !
Fluid one, fluid one !
The desert shall be washed for me.
Do not ignore me !'

8 (233)

To say the words :

'Fall, serpent that came forth from the Earth !
Fall, flame that came forth from Nun !
Fall down ! Crawl away !'

9 (234)

To say the words :

'On your face,
You on his coil !
Get down on your backbone,
You in your undergrowth !
Turn back because of me,
You rejoicing with her two faces.'

10 (235)

To say the words :

'You long one, beaten flank, beaten flank ! You have copulated with the two female guardians at the threshold of my praised sovereign.'

11 (236)

To say the words :

'Earthen One of the Courtyard,
<Trampled Porphyrite>, Foot-trampled,
Cord, son of Hifeget - that is your name !'

12 (237)

To say the words :

'The spittle is ended, what is in the (poison) sacs has fled to the house of its mother.
Monster, lie down !'

13 (238)

To say the words :

'The bread of your father is yours, You whose attack has missed ! Your own bread of your father is for You, You whose attack has missed ! The Gold of Jubilation, Apparent in Heat (as the Sun), that is your Bull, the strong one against whom this is done.'

14 (239)

To say the words :

'The White Crown has emerged and swallowed the Great One. The tongue of the White Crown gulped down the Great One, but the tongue was not seen.'

15 (240)

by the King

To say the words :

'Serpent, to the sky !
The centipede of Horus, to the Earth !
The cowherd, Horus, is stepping.
I, King Unas, have trodden on the path of Horus, unknowingly, not knowing.
On your face, You in his undergrowth !
Be dragged away, You who are in his cavern !
Meat for the pot of Horus,

which pervades the Earth !
O let the monster be off !'

16 (241)

To say the words :

'Spit of the wall !
Vomit of the brick !
What comes out of your mouth
has been turned back against yourself !'

17 (242)

To say the words :

'The flame has been extinguished !
No lamp can be found
in the house where the Ombite is.
The biting snake is all over the house of him
whom it would bite, hiding in it.'

18 (243)

To say the words :

'Two Hetes-sceptres,
two Hetes-sceptres,
belong to two Djema-ropes,
two Djema-ropes,
as trampled bread.

Lion, go away !

Whether You are here
or whether You are there,
servant, spit out !'

Offering Liturgy
North Wall

I Preliminary Purifications

all by the priest

19 (23)
purification by water

'Osiris, seize all those who hate King Unas *-pour water-* and who speak evil against his name. Thoth, go, seize him for Osiris.

Bring him who speaks evil against the name of King Unas. Put him in your hand.'

To say the words four times :

'Do not let go of him !
Beware, do not let go of him !' *-pour water-*

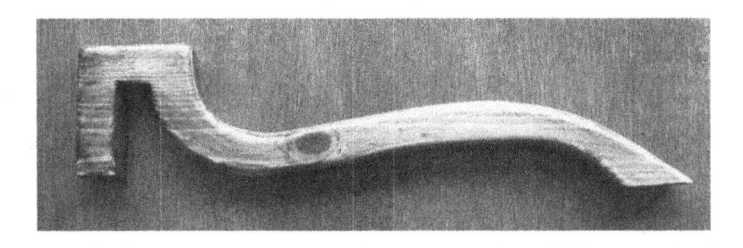

the 'Seb Ur' or 'Great Iron Tool'
used in the funerary *Ritual of Opening the Mouth*
of the mummy at the entrance of the tomb

20 (25)
censing Ka-rite

'Someone has gone with his Ka.
Horus has gone with his Ka.
Seth has gone with his Ka.
Thoth has gone with his Ka.'
To say the words four times.
-burning incense-

'The god has gone with his Ka.
Osiris goes with his Ka.

Eyes-Forward has gone with his Ka.
You also have gone with your Ka.

O King Unas,
the arm of your Ka is before You !
O King Unas,
the arm of your Ka is behind You !
O King Unas,
the foot of your Ka is before You !
O King Unas,
the foot of your Ka is behind You !

O Osiris King Unas,
I have given You the Eye of Horus !
May your face be adorned with it !

May the perfume of the Eye of Horus
diffuse over You !'

21 (32)
pouring of libation under the feet

'This is your libation, Osiris. This is your libation, O King Unas, have gone forth -*libation & two pellets of natron*- to your son, have gone forth to Horus. I have come and I bring You the Eye of Horus, that your heart may be refreshed with it. I bring it to You under your feet.

Take the outflow that comes out from You. Your heart will not be weary with it.'

To say the words four times :

'Come, (for) You have been invoked !'

22 (34)
mouth purification by Upper Egyptian natron

'Cream, cream,
splits open your mouth !

O King Unas,
-*Upper Egyptian natron of Nekheb, 5 pellets*-
taste its taste in front of them
of the divine chapels.

What Horus spits out is cream.
What Seth spits out is cream.
What reconciles the two gods is cream.'

To say the words four times :

'You are purified in the company of
the Followers of Horus.'

23 (35)
purification by Lower Egyptian natron

'Your purification is the purification of Horus.
Your purification is the purification of Seth.
-*Lower Egyptian natron of Shetpet, 5 pellets*-
Your purification is the purification of Thoth.
Your purification is the purification of the god.
Your purification is also among them.
Your mouth is the mouth of a sucking calf
on the day he is born.'

24 (36)
final censing and declaration of purity

'Your purification is the purification of Horus.
Your purification is the purification of Seth.
Your purification -*incense, one pellet*-
is the purification of Thoth.
Your purification is the purification of the god.
Your purification is the purification of your Ka.
Your purification is the purification of your purification,

and this purification of yours
also is among your brothers, the gods !
Your purification is on your mouth : You should clean
all your bones, and end what is against You.

O Osiris, I give You the Eye of Horus !
Provide your face with it, spread through.'

II Opening of the Mouth Rituals

1. Ritual of Opening the Mouth

25 (37)
the Peseshkef or Flint Spreader

'O King Unas, I have fastened your jaws spread for You.' -*the Peseshkef*-

26 (38)
the divine iron

'O Osiris King Unas, I split open your mouth for You.'
-*divine iron of Upper Egypt, 1 ingot ;*
divine iron of Lower Egypt, 1 ingot-

27 (39)
the Eye of Horus

'King Unas ! Take the Eye of Horus which went away : I have brought it to You that I might put it in your mouth.' -*Zeru-salt of Upper Egypt and Zeru-salt of Lower Egypt*-

28 (40)
the Shik of Osiris

'O King Unas,
take the Shiku-mineral of Osiris !' -*Shiku*-

29 (41)
the tip of the breast of Horus

'Take the tip of Horus' own breast !
Take what is for your mouth !' -*milk, 1 jar*-

30 (42)
the breast of Isis

'Take the breast of your sister Isis the milk-provider,
which You should take to your mouth.'
-*an empty Menza-jar*-

31 (32)
pouring of libation under the feet

'This is your libation, Osiris.
This is your libation,
O King Unas, have gone forth
-*libation & two pellets of natron*-
to your son, have gone forth to Horus.

I have come and I bring You the Eye of Horus, that
your heart may be refreshed with it.
I bring it to You under your feet.
Take the outflow that comes out from You.
Your heart will not be weary with it.'

To say the words four times :

'Come, (for) You have been invoked !'

2. Mouth-opening Meal

32 (43)
the Eye of Horus

'Take the two Eyes of Horus,
the black and the white.
Take them to your forehead,

that they may brighten your face.'
-the lifting up of a white jar and a black jar-

33 (44)
dedication of offerings to Re

'Re in the sky shall be pleased with You,
and he shall pacify the Two Lords for You.
The night is favorable to You.'
-a fresh bread-loaf-

'The Two Ladies are favorable to You.
Offerings have been brought to You.
Offerings is what You see.
Offerings is what You hear.
Offerings in front of You !
Offerings behind You !
Offerings are your portion !'

34 (45)
preparation of the mouth

'O Osiris King Unas,
take the white teeth of Horus,
which shall equip your mouth.'
-a bowl of 5 onions-heads-

35 (46)
offering for the Ka : first cake

To say the words four times :

'An offering which the King gives
for the Ka of King Unas.
O Osiris King Unas,
take the Eye of Horus,
your bread-loaf, and eat.'
-a bread-loaf of offering-

36 (47)
first cup

'O Osiris King Unas,
take the Eye of Horus,
which was taken from Seth and which You shall take to your mouth, and with which You should part your mouth.' -wine, a Hatjes jar of white quartzite stone-

37 (48)
second cup

'O Osiris King Unas,
part your mouth
with your full measure !'
-wine, a Hatjes jar of black quartzite stone-

38 (49)
third cup

'O Osiris King Unas,
take the <ferment> which comes from You !'
-beer, a Henet-bowl of black quartzite stone-

39 (50)
glorification of Re

'O Re ! Your dawning,
You in the sky, your dawning,
for King Unas,
Lord of All Things !
As all things belong to yourself,
let all things belong to the Ka of King Unas,
let all things belong to himself !'

*-the lifting up before him
of a sanctified offering-*

40 (51)
second cake

'King Unas !
Take the Eye of Horus,
which You should taste.'
-1 loin cake-

41 (52)
third cake

'(O) You interred !
(O) You of the dark !'
-1 porridge-loaf-

42 (53)
first meat

'King Unas ! Take the Eye of Horus,
which You should embrace.'
-1 kidney-

43 (54)
fourth cup

'King Unas ! Take the Eye of Horus,
which was taken from Seth and saved for You !
Part your mouth with it !'
-wine, a Henet-bowl of white quartzite stone-

44 (55)
fifth cup

'King Unas ! Take <the ferment>
that comes from Osiris !'
-beer, a Henet-bowl of black quartzite stone-

45 (56)
sixth cup

'King Unas ! Take the Eye of Horus,
rescued for You.
It will never escape from You !'
-*beer, an iron Henet-bowl*-

46 (57)
seventh cup

'King Unas !
Take the Eye of Horus,
provide yourself with it !'
-*beer, a blackened Henet-bowl*-

3. Anointment with Seven Oils

47 (72)
festival oil

'O Osiris King Unas,
I have filled your Eye with ointment.'
To say the words four times.
-*festival-scent oil*-

48 (73)
jubilation oil

'O Osiris King Unas,
take <the ferment> (which is) from his face.'
-*jubilation oil*-

49 (74)
pine oil

'O Osiris King Unas,
take the Eye of Horus,
on which he caused <devastation>.'
-*pine oil*-

50 (75)
rejoining oil

'O Osiris King Unas,
take the Eye of Horus, which he rejoined.'
-*rejoining oil*-

51 (76)
support oil

'O Osiris King Unas, take the Eye of Horus,
wherewith he got the gods.'
-*support oil*-

52 (77)
pine oil

'Ointment ! Ointment !
Where should You be ?
O You on the brow of Horus,
where should You be ?
-*first quality cedar oil*-
You were on the brow of Horus,
but I will put You
on the brow of this King Unas.
You shall give pleasure to him who wears You.
You shall make an Akh of him who wears You.
You shall cause him to have power in his body.
You shall put the dread of him in the eyes of all the
Akhs who shall look at him and everyone who shall
hear his name (as well).'

53 (78)
Libyan oil

'O Osiris King Unas,
I bring to You the Eye of Horus,
which he has taken to your brow.'
-*first quality Libyan oil*-

4. Presentation of Eyepaint

54 (79)
paint

To say the words four times :
'O Osiris King Unas,
the Eye of Horus has been painted sound on your face.'
-a bag of green eye-paint, a bag of black eye-paint-

5. Presentation of Linen

55 (81)
linen

'May You awake in peace !
Awake, Ta'it, in peace !
Awake, You of Ta'it-town, in peace !
-two roles of linen-

The Eye of Horus in Dep, in peace !
The Eye of Horus in the Mansions of the Red Crown,
in peace !

You who receive the working <women>, You who adorn the Great One of the carrying-chair, and cause the Two Lands to bow to this King Unas, like they bow to Horus, and cause the Two Lands to dread King Unas, like they dread Seth. May You sit in front of King Unas in his divinity, open his path at the head of the Akhs, that he may stand at the head of the Akhs like Anubis, at the fore of the Westerners. Forward ! To the front, with Osiris !'

6. Libation and Cleansing

56 (25)
censing Ka-rite

'Someone has gone with his Ka.
Horus has gone with his Ka.
Seth has gone with his Ka.
Thoth has gone with his Ka.'

To say the words four times.
-burning incense-

'The god has gone with his Ka.
Osiris goes with his Ka.
Eyes-Forward has gone with his Ka.
You also have gone with your Ka.

O King Unas,
the arm of your Ka is before You !
O King Unas,
the arm of your Ka is behind You !
O King Unas,
the foot of your Ka is before You !
O King Unas,
the foot of your Ka is behind You !

O Osiris King Unas,
I have given You the Eye of Horus !
May your face be adorned with it !
May the perfume of the Eye of Horus
diffuse over You !'

57 (32)
pouring of libation under the feet

'This is your libation, Osiris.
This is your libation, O King Unas, have gone forth -
libation & two pellets of natron-
to your son, have gone forth to Horus.'

I have come and I bring You the Eye of Horus,
that your heart may be refreshed with it.
I bring it to You under your feet.

Take the outflow that comes out from You.
Your heart will not be weary with it.'

To say the words four times :

'Come, (for) You have been invoked !'

III Offering Banquet

1. Preparation of the Offering Table

58 (82)

'Thoth came with it to him.
He has come forth to him
with the Eye of Horus.'
-an offering table-

59 (83)

'Give him the Eye of Horus,
that he may become satisfied with it.'
-O come with the king's offering !-

60 (84)

'O Osiris King Unas,
take the Eye of Horus
with which he became satisfied.'
-the king's offering, twice-

61 (85)

'O Osiris King Unas,
take the Eye of Horus
and be satisfied with it.'
-two offering slabs of the broad hall-

62 (86)

To say the words :

'Cause it to turn back to You !'
-Sit down ! Be silent !
The King's invocation-offering-

63 (87)

'O Osiris King Unas,
take the Eye of Horus
and absorb it into your mouth.'
-the mouth-washing meal,
1 loaf of bread, 1 jug of beer-

64 (88)

'O Osiris King Unas,
take the Eye of Horus,
prevent him from trampling it.'
-1 loaf of trampled bread-

65 (89)

'O Osiris King Unas,
take the Eye of Horus which he pulled out.'
-1 bowl of pulled bread-

66 (90)

'O Osiris King Unas,
take the Eye of Horus,
for little is that which Seth has eaten of it.'
-1 jar of strong ale-

67 (91)

'O Osiris King Unas,
take the Eye of Horus
which they have <reft> from him.'
-1 jar of Henemes-drink-

68 (92)

'O Osiris King Unas,
take the Eye of Horus, lift it to your face.'
-the lifting up of 1 loaf of bread and
1 Henet-bowl of beer-

69 (93)

'Lift up your face, O Osiris.
Lift up your face, O King Unas,
whose Akh goes !

Lift up your face, O King Unas,
be strong and effective.
Look at what has come from You,
striking the one who is netted in it.
Wash yourself King Unas, and
part your mouth with the Eye of Horus.

You shall summon your Ka as Osiris,
and he shall protect You
from every wrath of the dead.

King Unas, take to yourself this bread of yours,
which is the Eye of Horus.'

70 (94)

'O Osiris King Unas,
take the Eye of Horus
with which You have <refreshed> yourself.'
-a Shenes-loaf-

71 (95)

'Provide yourself with <the ferment>
which comes from You.'
-four times, a meal, 1 loaf, 1 jug of beer-

72 (96)

'O Osiris King Unas,
take the one of the shank,
the Eye of Horus.'
-1 bowl with a shank of meat-

2. Cleansing the mouth

73 (108)

'O Osiris King Unas,
gather to yourself
the water that is in it.'
-2 bowls of water-

74 (109)

'O Osiris King Unas,
take the Eye of Horus,
which cleansed his mouth.'
-2 bowls of cleansing natron-

75 (110)

'O Osiris King Unas,
take the Eye of Horus,
gather it to your mouth.'

*-the mouth-washing meal,
1 loaf of bread, 1 jug of beer-*

3. Bread and Onions

76 (111)

'O Osiris King Unas,
take the Eye of Horus which Seth trampled.'
-1 loaf of trampled bread-

77 (112)

'O Osiris King Unas,
take the Eye of Horus which he pulled out.'
-1 bowl of pulled bread-

78 (113)

'O Osiris King Unas,
acquire what should be on You.'
-2 loaves of Hetj-bread-

79 (114)

'O Osiris King Unas,
I bring to You what [resembles] your face.'
-2 loaves of cone bread-

80 (115)

'O Osiris King Unas,
I have set your Eye in place.'
-4 loaves of taste bread-

81 (116)

'O Osiris King Unas,
take the Eye of Horus !
Prevent him from suffering because of it.'
-4 loaves of flat beer bread-

82 (117)

'O Osiris King Unas,
receive what should be on You.'

To say the words four times.
-4 loaves of Shenes bread-

83 (118)

'O Osiris King Unas,
take your Eye, take possession of it.'
To say the words four times.
-a bowl with 4 loaves of in-the-Earth-bread-

84 (119)

'O Osiris King Unas,
take the Eye of Horus,
which he <carried off>.'
-a bowl of 4 Henefu-breads-

85 (120)

'O Osiris King Unas,
take the Eye of Horus,
do not let it <spring up>.'
-a bowl of 4 Hebennet-breads-

86 (121)

'O Osiris King Unas,
take the Eye of Horus,
which he has pulled out.'
-a bowl of 4 wheat breads-

87 (122)

'O Osiris King Unas,
take the Eye of Horus,
put for You in your mouth.'
-a bowl of 4 truncated Idetet-breads-

88 (123)

'O Osiris King Unas,
take the Eye of Horus, your bread loaf and eat.'
-4 bread loaves-

89 (124)

'O Osiris King Unas,
take the Eye of Horus,
which he has pulled out.'
-*a bowl of 4 pieces of roast meat*-

90 (125)

'O Osiris King Unas,
I bring to You his white,
sound teeth.'
-*a bowl of 4 onions*-

4. Beef and Poultry

91 (126)

'O Osiris King Unas, here is the one
who stole the Eye of Horus.'
-*1 bowl with a foreleg*-

92 (127)

'O Osiris King Unas, dance !
 Geb will not do wrong to his heir who inherits.'
-*1 bowl with a haunch*-

93 (128)

'O Osiris King Unas,
take the Eye of Horus,
which You should embrace.'
-*1 bowl of kidneys*-

94 (129)

'O Osiris King Unas,
accept the one of the shank,

the Eye of Horus.'
-1 bowl with a shank of meat-

95 (130)

'O Osiris King Unas,
take those who rebelled against You.'

To say the words four times.
-a bowl of 4 ribs-

96 (131)

'O Osiris King Unas,
take your <assailant>.'

To say the words four times.
-1 bowl of roasted meat-

97 (132)

'O Osiris King Unas,
take the Eye of Horus,
go toward it.'
-1 bowl of liver-

98 (133)

'O Osiris King Unas,
take the Eye of Horus
against which he went.'
-1 bowl of spleen-

99 (134)

'O Osiris King Unas,
take the Eye of Horus
which is from his forehead.'
-1 bowl of belly meat-

100 (135)

'O Osiris King Unas,
take the Eye of Horus
which is from Seth's forehead.'
-1 bowl of breast meat-

101 (136)

'O Osiris King Unas,
take the <severed> heads of the Followers of Seth.'
-1 bowl of goose-

102 (137)

'O Osiris King Unas,
take <all> of this heart.'
To say the words four times.
-1 bowl of white-fronted goose-

103 (138)

'O Osiris King Unas,
take the Eye of Horus, which he has brought.'
-1 bowl of duck-

104 (139)

'O Osiris King Unas,
take the one who came to settle them.'
-1 bowl of grey goose-

105 (140)

'O Osiris King Unas,
take the Eye of Horus !
Prevent him from having pain in it.'
-1 bowl of pigeon-

5. Bread

106 (141)

'O Osiris King Unas,
take the Eye of Horus
which he pulled out.'
-1 loaf of warm bread-

107 (142)

'O Osiris King Unas,
take the Eye of Horus,
for it cannot be cut off from You.'
-2 loaves of cut bread-

108 (143)

'O Osiris King Unas,
the Eye of Horus
is allotted to You.'
-a bowl of 2 loaves of Nepat-bread-

109 (144)

'O Osiris King Unas,
take the Eye of Horus,
the water of which he caused to suffer.'
-a bowl of 2 loaves of Meset-bread-

6. Drinks

110 (145)

'O Osiris King Unas,
take the Eye of Horus,
for little is that which Seth has eaten of it.'
-2 bowls of strong ale-

111 (146)

'O Osiris King Unas,
take the eye of Horus,
(for) they come, who have <torn>
a piece from it.'
-2 bowls of whipped cream-

112 (147)

'O Osiris King Unas,
take the Eye of Horus
which they <reft> from him.'
-2 bowls of Henemes-bear-

113 (148)

'O Osiris King Unas,
provide yourself with <the ferment>
which comes out of You.'
-2 bowls of beer-

114 (149)

'O Osiris King Unas,
provide yourself with <the ferment>
which comes out of You.'
-2 bowls of date beer-

115 (150)

'O Osiris King Unas,
provide yourself with <the ferment>
which comes out of You.'
-2 bowls of Pekh(a)-beer-

116 (151)

'O Osiris King Unas,
provide yourself with <the ferment>

which comes out of You.'
-*2 bowls of bowland beer-*

117 (152)

'O Osiris King Unas,
take the breast of Horus which they offer.'
-*2 bowls of fig drink-*

118 (153)

'O Osiris King Unas,
part your mouth with it.'
-*2 bowls of Delta wine-*

119 (154)

'O Osiris King Unas, take the Eye of Horus which they spat out ! Prevent him from swallowing it.'
-*2 jars of Abesh-wine-*

120 (155)

'O Osiris King Unas,
take the pupil in the Eye of Horus,
part your mouth with it.'
-*2 bowls of Buto wine-*

121 (156)

'O Osiris King Unas, take the Eye of Horus
which he has fished up,
(and) part your mouth with it.'
-*2 bowls of Mariut wine-*

122 (157)

'O Osiris King Unas,
take the Eye of Horus !

It will not separate itself from You.'
-*2 bowls of Pelusium wine*-

7. Fruits

123 (158)

'O Osiris King Unas, take the Eye of Horus
as it <springs up>.'
-*2 bowls of Hebennet*-

124 (159)

'O Osiris King Unas,
take the Eye of Horus
which he <carried off>.'
-*2 bowls of Khenfu*-

125 (160)

'O Osiris King Unas,
take the Eye of Horus
which he took from Seth.'
-*2 bowls of Ished-berries*-

126 (161)

'O Osiris King Unas,
take the white Eye of Horus
and prevent him
from wearing it as a headband.'
-*2 bowls of white Seshet*-

127 (162)

'O Osiris King Unas,
take the green Eye of Horus
and prevent him
 from wearing it as a headband.'
-*2 bowls of green Seshet*-

128 (163)

'O Osiris King Unas,
take the Eye of Horus
and prevent him from tearing it out.'
-2 bowls of roasted wheat-

129 (164)

'O Osiris King Unas,
take the Eye of Horus
and prevent him from tearing it out.'
-2 bowls of roasted barley-

130 (165)

'O Osiris King Unas,
take the Eye of Horus,
<it is slipping>.'
-2 bowls of Ba(ba)t-

131 (166)

'O Osiris King Unas, take the Eye of Horus
which they have licked.'
-2 bowls of Sidder fruit-

132 (167)

'O Osiris King Unas,
open your eyes and see with them.'
-2 bowls of Sidder bread-

133 (168)

'O Osiris King Unas, take the Eye of Horus
and prevent him from netting it.'
-2 bowls of carob beans-

8. Vegetables

134 (169)

'O Osiris King Unas, take the sweet Eye of Horus,
return it to yourself.'
-2 bowls of all kinds of sweet stalk-

135 (170)

'O Osiris King Unas,
take the Eye of Horus,
allot it to yourself.'
-2 bowls of all kind of young plant-

9. Dedication of Offerings

136 (171)

'O Osiris King Unas,
may what You have endure for You with You !'
-dedication of the offerings-

Voyage to the Duat
South Wall

The King enters the Duat

137 (213)
the King on the throne of Osiris

by the priest

'O King Unas !
You have not gone away dead !
You have gone away alive !

Sit upon the throne of Osiris.
Your Power-scepter in your hand,
that You may give orders to the living.

Your Lotus-bud scepter in your hand,
that You may give orders to those
whose seats are hidden.

Your lower arms are of Atum.
Your upper arms are of Atum.
Your belly is of Atum.
Your back is of Atum.
Your rear is of Atum.
Your legs are of Atum.
Your face is of Anubis.

The Mounds of Horus shall serve You.
The Mounds of Seth shall serve You.'

138 (214)
at the Head of the Westerners

by the priest

'O King Unas,
beware of the Lake (of Fire) !'

To say the words four times.

'The messengers of your Ka come for You.
The messengers of your father come for You.

The messengers of Re come for You, (saying) :

"Go after your Sun and cleanse yourself, for your bones are those of the divine falcon-goddesses who are in the sky. May You be beside the god. May You leave your house and ascend to your son."

May You <fetter> anyone who shall speak evilly against the name of King Unas !

Go up, for Geb has committed him to a low estate in the town of the pregnant one, so that he may flee and sink down weary.

But You shall bathe in the cool water of the stars ! You shall board (the sunboat) upon ropes of iron, on the shoulders of Horus in his name of "Him who is in Sokar's boat".

The Sun-folk will cry out to You once the Imperishable Stars have raised You aloft.

Ascend to the place where your father is, to the place where Geb is, that he will give You that which is on the brow of Horus, so that You shall come an Akh thereby, take control thereby and that You shall be at the head of the Westerners thereby.'

The King protected by Atum

139 (215)
healing rivals and becoming completed

by the priest

'O King Unas, your messengers have gone, your heralds have run to your father, to Atum (to say for You) :

"Atum, raise him up to You, enclose him within your arms. There is no star-god who has no companion : I am our companion.

Look at me, as You have seen the shapes of the children of their fathers, who know their spell, who are Imperishable Stars ! See (in me) the two who are in the Palace - that is, Horus and Seth."

Spit on the face of Horus for him, that You may remove the injury against him ! Pick up the testicles of Seth, that You may remove his mutilation. That one has been born for You, this one has been conceived for You, for You have given birth to Horus, in his name of "Him at whom the Earth quakes and the sky trembles". This one has no mutilation, that one has no injury. That one has no injury, this one has no mutilation. You (Unas) have no injury, You have no mutilation.

You have been born, O Horus, for Osiris, and You have more Ba than he. You have more power than he. You have been conceived, O Seth, for Geb, and You have more Ba than he. You have more power than he.

There is no own seed of a god that has gone (from life), and You, his own, will not go. Re-Atum will not give You to Osiris, and he will not claim your mind, nor have power over your heart. Re-Atum will not give You to Horus, and he will not claim your mind, nor have power over your heart.

O Osiris, You cannot control him,
your son cannot control him !
O Horus, You shall never have power over him,
nor shall your father have power over him !

You belong, So-and-so, to that god of whom the Twin Children of Atum said : "You are distinguished", say they, "in your identity of a god".

You shall become completed to every god !
Your head is Horus of the Duat,

O Imperishable Star.
Your face is Eyes-Forward,
O Imperishable Star.
Your ears are the Twin Children of Atum,
O Imperishable Star.
Your eyes are the Twin Children of Atum,

O Imperishable Star.
Your nose is the Jackal,
O Imperishable Star.
Your teeth are Sopdu,
O Imperishable Star.
Your hands are [Hapy] and Duamutef.

When You demand to ascend to the sky, You ascend !
Your feet are Imseti and Qebsenuf. When You demand to descend to the Lower Sky, You descend ! Your limbs are the Twin Children of Atum.

O Imperishable Star.
You will not perish,
your Ka will not perish : You are a Ka !'

The Midnight Mystery

140 (216)
King Unas encircled in the Nightboat

by the King

To say the words :

'I have come to You, O Nephthys !
I have come to You, O Nightboat !
I have come to You,
O Pilot-covered-in-Red !

I have come to You,
O Place-where-the Kas-are-remembered !
May You remember me, this King Unas !

Orion has become encircled by the Duat, as the Living One became pure in the horizon.
So this has become encircled by the Duat, as the Living One became pure in the horizon.

I, this King Unas,
has become encircled by the Duat, as the Living One
became pure in the horizon.

I have become Akh for them !
I have grown cool for them !
Inside the arms of my father,
inside the arms of Atum !'

141 (217)
King Unas gathering with Atum

by the priest

To say the words :

'Re-Atum, this King Unas has come to You, an imperishable Akh, Lord of <the Affairs> of the Place of the Four Papyrus Pillars. Your son has come to You, this King Unas has come to You. You shall both traverse the sky, after gathering in the darkness (of the Duat) ! May You rise from the horizon, from the place in which You have both become Akh !

Seth and Nephthys, go, and proclaim to the gods of the Nile Valley as well as their Akhs : "This King Unas has come, an imperishable Akh. If he wishes You to die, You will die ! If he wishes You to live, You will live !"

Re-Atum, this King Unas has come to You, an imperishable Akh, Lord of <the Affairs> of the Place of the Four Papyrus Pillars. Your son has come to You, this King Unas has come to You. You shall both traverse the sky, after gathering in the darkness (of the Duat) ! May You rise from the horizon, from the place in which You have both become Akh !

Osiris and Isis, go, and proclaim to the gods of Lower Egypt and their Akhs :

"This King Unas has come, an imperishable Akh, as one to be worshipped, (Osiris) who is in charge of the inundation.

Worship him, You Akhs who are in the waters ! Whom he wishes to live will live ! Whom he wishes to die will die !"

Re-Atum, this King Unas has come to You, an imperishable Akh, Lord of <the Affairs> of the Place of the Four Papyrus Pillars. Your son has come to You, this King Unas has come to You. You shall both traverse the sky, after gathering in the darkness (of the Duat) ! May You rise from the horizon, from the place in which You have both become Akh !

Thoth, go, and proclaim to gods of the West and their Akhs : "This King Unas has come indeed, an imperishable Akh, arrayed on the neck as Anubis at the head of the Western Mountain, that he may claim hearts (and) have power over hearts. Whom he wishes to live will live ! Whom he wishes to die will die !"

Re-Atum, this King Unas has come to You, an imperishable Akh, Lord of <the Affairs> of the Place of the Four Papyrus Pillars. Your son has come to You, this King Unas has come to You. You shall both traverse the sky, after gathering in the darkness (of the Duat) ! May You rise from the horizon, from the place in which You have both become Akh !

Horus, go, and proclaim
to Bas of the East and their Akhs :

"This King Unas has come indeed,
an imperishable Akh.
Whom he wishes to live will live !
Whom he wishes to die will die !"

O Re-Atum, your son has come to You, King Unas has come to You.

Raise him up to You, enclose him in your arms, for he is the son of your body for ever !'

Osirian rebirth of the King

142 (218)
King Unas presented to Osiris

by the priest

To say the words :

'O Osiris, this King Unas has come indeed, the <fledgling> of the Ennead, an imperishable Akh.

He will claim minds, take away Kas and bestow Kas as what he reckons, including whomever he summons to his side or appeals to him. There is none who will be excluded without his bread, without his Kas bread, deprived of his bread.

Geb has spoken and it has come from the mouth of the Ennead :

"O falcon who succeeds (his father) in acquiring (the throne)", they said : "You are a Ba and in control !"

This King Unas has come indeed, the <fledgling> of the Ennead, an imperishable Akh, who surpassed You and surpasses You, wearier than You and greater than You, sounder than You and more acclaimed than You, and your time here is no more.

It is what Seth and Thoth have done, your two brothers who do not mourn You.

Isis and Nephthys, come together, come together!
Unite, unite! This King Unas has come indeed, the
<fledgling> of the Ennead, an imperishable Akh.

The Westerners who are on Earth belong to this King
Unas. This King Unas has come indeed, the <fledgling>
of the Ennead, an imperishable Akh.

The Easterners who are on Earth belong to this King
Unas. This King Unas has come indeed, the <fledgling>
of the Ennead, an imperishable Akh.

The Southerners who are on Earth belong to this King
Unas. This King Unas has come indeed, the <fledgling>
of the Ennead, an imperishable Akh.

The Northerners who are on Earth belong to this King
Unas. This King Unas has come indeed, the <fledgling>
of the Ennead, an imperishable Akh.

Those who are in the Lower Sky belong to this King
Unas. This King Unas has come indeed, the <fledgling>
of the Ennead, an imperishable Akh.'

143 (219)
Litany of identification with the Living Osiris

by the priest

To say the words :

'Atum, this Osiris here is your son, whom You have
caused to be restored that he may live :

He lives! This King Unas lives!
He is not dead!
This King Unas lives!
He is not destroyed!
This King Unas is not destroyed!
He has not been judged!

This King Unas has not been judged !
He judges. This King Unas judges !

Shu, this Osiris here is your son, whom You have caused to be restored that he may live.

He lives ! This King Unas lives ! He is not dead ! This King Unas lives ! He is not destroyed ! This King Unas is not destroyed ! He has not been judged ! This King Unas has not been judged ! He judges. This King Unas judges.

Tefnut, this Osiris here is your son, whom You have caused to be restored that he may live.

He lives ! This King Unas lives ! He is not dead ! This King Unas lives ! He is not destroyed ! This King Unas is not destroyed ! He has not been judged ! This King Unas has not been judged ! He judges. This King Unas judges.

Geb, this Osiris here is your son, whom You have caused to be restored that he may live.

He lives ! This King Unas lives ! He is not dead ! This King Unas lives ! He is not destroyed ! This King Unas is not destroyed ! He has not been judged ! This King Unas has not been judged ! He judges. This King Unas judges.

Nut, this Osiris here is your son, whom You have caused to be restored that he may live.

He lives ! This King Unas lives ! He is not dead ! This King Unas lives ! He is not destroyed ! This King Unas is not destroyed ! He has not been judged ! This King Unas has not been judged ! He judges. This King Unas judges.

Isis, this Osiris here is your brother, whom You have caused to be restored that he may live.

He lives ! This King Unas lives ! He is not dead ! This King Unas lives ! He is not destroyed ! This King Unas is not destroyed ! He has not been judged ! This King Unas has not been judged ! He judges. This King Unas judges. Seth, this Osiris here is your brother, who has been caused to be restored that he may live and punish You.

He lives ! This King Unas lives ! He is not dead ! This King Unas lives ! He is not destroyed ! This King Unas is not destroyed ! He has not been judged ! This King Unas has not been judged ! He judges. This King Unas judges.

Nephthys, this Osiris here is your brother, whom You have caused to be restored that he may live.

He lives ! This King Unas lives ! He is not dead ! This King Unas lives ! He is not destroyed ! This King Unas is not destroyed ! He has not been judged ! This King Unas has not been judged ! He judges. This King Unas judges.

Thoth, this Osiris here is your brother, who has been caused to be restored that he may live and punish You.

He lives ! This King Unas lives ! He is not dead ! This King Unas lives ! He is not destroyed ! This King Unas is not destroyed ! He has not been judged ! This King Unas has not been judged ! He judges. This King Unas judges.

Horus, this Osiris here is your father, whom You have caused to be restored that he may live.

He lives ! This King Unas lives ! He is not dead ! This King Unas lives ! He is not destroyed ! This King Unas is not destroyed ! He has not been judged ! This King Unas has not been judged ! He judges. This King Unas judges.

Great Ennead, this one here is Osiris, whom You have caused to be restored that he may live.

He lives ! This King Unas lives ! He is not dead ! This King Unas lives ! He is not destroyed !

This King Unas is not destroyed ! He has not been judged ! This King Unas has not been judged ! He judges. This King Unas judges !

Lesser Ennead, this one here is Osiris, whom You have caused to be restored that he may live.

He lives ! This King Unas lives ! He is not dead ! This King Unas lives ! He is not destroyed ! This King Unas is not destroyed ! He has not been judged ! This King Unas has not been judged ! He judges. This King Unas judges.

Nunet, this Osiris here is your son, of whom You said:

"Someone has been born to me.", You said, and You wiped his mouth for him after his mouth had been parted by his beloved son Horus and his limbs numbered by the gods.

He lives ! This King Unas lives ! He is not dead ! This King Unas lives ! He is not destroyed ! This King Unas is not destroyed ! He has not been judged ! This King Unas has not been judged ! He judges. This King Unas judges.

In your name of Dweller in Heliopolis, who endures in his necropolis.

He lives ! This King Unas lives ! He is not dead ! This King Unas lives ! He is not destroyed ! This King Unas is not destroyed ! He has not been judged ! This King Unas has not been judged ! He judges. This King Unas judges.

In your name of Dweller in Busiris, chief of his nomes.

He lives ! This King Unas lives ! He is not dead ! This King Unas lives ! He is not destroyed ! This King Unas is not destroyed ! He has not been judged ! This King Unas has not been judged ! He judges. This King Unas judges.

In your name of Dweller in the Mansion of Selket, the Ka At Rest.

He lives ! This King Unas lives ! He is not dead ! This King Unas lives ! He is not destroyed ! This King Unas is not destroyed ! He has not been judged ! This King Unas has not been judged ! He judges. This King Unas judges.

In your name of Dweller in the divine booth, who is in the censing, the one of the coffer, the chest and the sack.

He lives ! This King Unas lives ! He is not dead ! This King Unas lives ! He is not destroyed ! This King Unas is not destroyed ! He has not been judged ! This King Unas has not been judged ! He judges. This King Unas judges.

In your name of him who is in the White Palace of Laurel wood.

He lives ! This King Unas lives ! He is not dead ! This King Unas lives ! He is not destroyed ! This King Unas is not destroyed ! He has not been judged ! This King Unas has not been judged ! He judges. This King Unas judges.

In your name of Dweller in Orion, with your season in the sky and your season on Earth.

O Osiris, turn your face and look on this King Unas, for your seed which issued from You is effective :

He lives ! This King Unas lives ! He is not dead ! This King Unas lives ! He is not destroyed ! This King Unas is not destroyed ! He has not been judged ! This King Unas has not been judged ! He judges. This King Unas judges.

In your name of Dweller in Buto, may your arms be about the meal, your daughter,

143 (219)
litany of identification with the Living Osiris
(continued on the East Wall)

provide yourself with it.

He lives ! This King Unas lives ! He is not dead ! This King Unas lives ! He is not destroyed ! This King Unas is not destroyed ! He has not been judged ! This King Unas has not been judged ! He judges. This King Unas judges.

In your name of Dweller in the Mansion of the Eldest of Bulls, may your arms be about the meal, your daughter, provide yourself with it.

He lives ! This King Unas lives ! He is not dead ! This King Unas lives ! He is not destroyed ! This King Unas is not destroyed ! He has not been judged ! This King Unas has not been judged ! He judges. This King Unas judges.

In your name of Dweller in Hermopolis of the South, may your arms be about the meal, your daughter, provide yourself with it.

He lives ! This King Unas lives ! He is not dead ! This King Unas lives ! He is not destroyed ! This King Unas is not destroyed ! He has not been judged ! This King Unas has not been judged ! He judges. This King Unas judges.

In your name of Dweller in Hermopolis of the North, may your arms be about the meal, your daughter, provide yourself with it.

He lives ! This King Unas lives ! He is not dead ! This King Unas lives ! He is not destroyed ! This King Unas is not destroyed ! He has not been judged ! This King Unas has not been judged ! He judges. This King Unas judges. In your name of Dweller in the Town of Lakes. What You have eaten, an Eye, your belly shall grow round from it, your son Horus releasing it for You (so) that You may live from it.

He lives ! This King Unas lives ! He is not dead ! This King Unas lives ! He is not destroyed ! This King Unas is not destroyed ! He has not been judged ! This King Unas has not been judged ! He judges. This King Unas judges.

Your body is the body of this King Unas, your flesh is the flesh of this King Unas, your bones are the bones of this King Unas : You will go (from life) should this King Unas go. Should this King Unas go, You will go !'

Service of the Crown

144 (220)
opening of the shrine

The doors of the horizon has been opened, its bolts have drawn back.

by the priest to the crown

'He has come to You,
Red Crown !
He has come to You,
Fiery Serpent !
He has come to You,
Great One !
He has come to You,
Great of Magic,
pure for You and fearing You !

May You be pleased with him, may You be pleased with his purity, and may You be pleased with his speech when he says to You : "How fine You look, content, renewed, and rejuvenated, for the god who is the father of the gods has given You birth !"

He has come to You,
Great of Magic : he is Horus
encircled by the protection of his Eye,
the Great of Magic !'

145 (221)
opening of the shrine

prayer by the King

'O Red Crown !
O Curl !
O Great Crown !
O Crown Great of Magic !
O Fiery Serpent !
Grant that the dread of me
be like the dread of You !

Grant that the fear of me
be like the fear of You !

Grant that the acclaim of me
be like the acclaim of You !

Grant that the love of me
be like the love of You !

Set my Aba-scepter at the head of the living, (set) my [Power-scepter] at the head of the Akhs, and grant that my sword prevails over my foes. O Curl ! [You] have emerged [in me, so have I emerged in You.']

reply by the Red Crown

'The Great Thing [has given You birth], the Firstborn's Cobra goddess thing has adorned You, the Firstborn's Cobra goddess thing has given You birth, the Great Thing [has adorned You], for You are Horus, encircled by the protection of his Eye !'

Commendations to Re

146 (222)
joining the ongoing circuit of Re

by the priest

To say the words :

'You shall stand up on it, this Earth [which issued from Atum, this spittle], which issued from Kheprer.

Evolve on it, become exalted on it, and your father will see You, Re will see You.'

prayer by the King

'I have come to You, my father,
I have come to You, O Re.
I have come to You, my father,
I have come to You, O Downcast.
I have come to You, my father,
I have come to You, O Fertilizer.
I have come to You, my father,
I have come to You, O Rager.
I have come to You, my father,
I have come to You, O Great Wild Bull.
I have come to You, my father,
I have come to You,
O Great Reedfloat-user.
I have come to You, my father,
I have come to You, O Sopdu.
I have come to You, my father,
I have come to You, O Sharp-teeth.

Grant that I, King Unas, may seize the Cool Waters and receive the horizon. Grant that I may rule the Nine and provide for the Ennead.

Place the Crook in my hand, that the head of the Delta and the Nile Valley may be bowed.

I charge my opponent and stand up over the Great One as his greater, (as) the one Nephthys has blessed, for I have captured my opponent, (saying) :

"You have provide yourself with the Great of Magic, (as) Seth dwelling in Ombos, Lord of Upper Egypt. Nothing has been is lost to You, nothing has been <wanting> to You. For see, You are more Ba and more in control than the gods of Upper Egypt and their Akhs, You whom the Pregnant One ejected, and You have <illumined> the night, equipped as Seth, whose raw (testicles) were pulled off."

(As) one Isis has blessed, (saying) :

"You have provided yourself as Horus the Youthful ! Indeed, nothing is lost to You, nothing has <ceased> for You ! For see, You are more Ba and more in control than the gods of the North and their Akhs."'

by the priest

'Cast off your impurity for Atum in [Heliopolis and go down with him.] Assign the <needs> of the Lower Sky and succeed to the thrones of Nun.

You shall come into being with your father Atum, You shall go up on high with your father Atum, You shall rise with your father Atum, and may (your) <needs> be released from You.

Head to (Nut), the Lady of Heliopolis in the sedan chair. Go up, open your way by means of the bones of Shu, that the inside of your mother Nut's arms may enfold You.

You shall become pure in the horizon and get rid of your impurity in the Lakes of Shu.

Ascend and descend !
Descend with Re,
one of the dusk with
the One Who Was Cast Down.
Ascend and descend !
Ascend with Re,
rise with the Great Float-user.
Ascend and descend !
Descend with Nephthys,
sink into darkness with the Nightboat.
Ascend and descend !
Ascend with Isis,
rise with the Dayboat.

You shall have power over your body, for You have no hindrance. Having been born to (be) Horus, and conceived to (be) Seth. Having become pure in the Western nome, having received your purification in the Bubastite nome with your father, with Atum.

You have come into being, You have gone up on high, and You have become effective. It has become pleasant for You inside your father's arms, inside Atum's arms.

Atum, elevate this King Unas to You,
encircle him inside your arms,
for he is your son of your body, forever.'

Calling the King

147 (223)
the King is called back

by the priest

'Hey ! Turn around !
Ah ! Ah !
O King Unas !

Stand up and sit down to a thousand of bread, a thousand of beer, roast meat, your rib-meat from the slaughterhouse, and pulled bread from the broad hall.

As the god is provided with a divine offering, King Unas is provided with this his bread.

You have Come to your Ba, Osiris, Ba among the Akhu, in control in his places, whom the Ennead tend in the Mansion of the Prince.

O King Unas !

Elevate yourself up to me, betake yourself toward me : do not be far from me, tomb-dweller, and turn toward me.

I have given You the Eye of Horus.
I have allotted it to You,
may it <endure> for You with You.

O King Unas !
Arise, receive this your bread from my hand !
O King Unas !
I will be an attendant for You !'

148 (224)
happy and changed

by the priest

To say the words :

'Hey, You King Unas !
Turn about, You King Unas !
You have gone,
that You may govern the Mounds of Horus !
You have gone,
that You may govern the Mounds of Seth !

You have gone,
that You may govern the Mounds of Osiris !

An offering which the King grants to all your insignia wherever You may be : your Lotus-bud sceptre at the head of the living, your staff at the head of the Akhs, as Anubis at the fore of the Westerners, as Andjeti at the fore of the eastern nomes.

How happy is your condition
as You become Akh,
O King Unas,
among your brothers the gods !
How changed !
How changed,
You whom your child tended.
Beware of your limit in the Earth.
Put on your body and come to them !'
-*four times*-

Foodspells for King Unas the Living Horus
East Gable

The King eats the food of the gods

149 (204)
nourishment by Osiris

by the priest

'The hoers rejoice, the heart of those who cleanse the breast became fully uplifted, when they swallowed the Eye of Horus, the healthy one which is in Heliopolis.

The little finger of King Unas, pulls out what is in the navel of Osiris.

King Unas will not thirst, he will not hunger : it will not be against the heart of King Unas.

His arms drive away his hunger.
Become awash (with joy) !
Make the hearts full !'

150 (205)
the Great Bull cared for

by the priest

To say the words :

'O You who preside over the baked foods.
O You who belong to the flood.

Commend King Unas to Fetekte, the cupbearer of Re, whom Re has commended to himself, that Re may commend him to the one in charge of provisioning for this year, that they may seize barley and give him beer, that they may grasp emmer and give him bread. For to King Unas, his father is the one who gave barley and beer, Re is the one who gave emmer and bread.

For he is the Great Bull who smote Kenzet. For King Unas is he who has the five portions of bread, drink and cakes in the enclosure : a triad is for the sky with Re and a pair is for the Earth with the Two Enneads. He belongs to the one who was set loose : he is the one who was let loose. He belongs to the one who is seen : he is the one who is seen.

O Re, it is better with him today than yesterday !

For King Unas has mated with moisture.
King Unas has kissed dryness.
King Unas has joined with fertility.

King Unas has copulated with the young girl of his care when grain and <fluids> were absent, and the young girl of the care of King Unas is the one who will give bread to King Unis and make it better for him today.'

151 (207)
King Unas calls to the Eye for a meal

by the King

To say the words :

'A meal for me, O knife-sharpener !
A meal for me, O knife-sharpener !
A meal, You in Re's Eye !

A meal for me,
You with access to (Re's) boat,
You in the God's-Eye (boat) !

O cupbearer, bring water !
Light the fire (for) a joint
among the roast meat !'
-4 handfuls of water-

152 (209)
King Unas is provided with bread

by the priest

To say the words :

'Shu is fresh !
King Unas does not acquire his things.
King Unas is fresh !

Shu does not acquire his things.
The eastern fetchers shall repeat :
"It is your bread."'

153 (210)
King Unas is protected against inversion

by the King

To say the words :

'Awake, O Parter !
Be high, O Thoth !

Awake, You sleepers !

Rise up, You dwellers in Kenzet, who are before the Great Heron that comes from the [garden], Path-Parter who comes from the tamarisk.

My mouth is pure, the Two Enneads have censed me, and pure indeed is this tongue which is in my mouth.

What I, King Unas, detest is faeces.
I reject urine.
I detest my own abomination.

What I detest is these two : I will never eat the abomination of these two, just as Seth rejects the two <companions> that cross the sky.

Re and Thoth, take me with You, that I, King Unas, may eat of what You eat, that I may drink of what You drink, that I may live on what You live on, that I may sit on what You sit on, that I may be strong through that whereby You are strong, that I may sail in that in which You sail. My pavilion is plaited with reeds, my drink-supply is in the Field of Offerings, my food-offerings are among You, gods ; my water is wine like that of Re, and I go round the sky like Re, I traverse the sky like Thoth.'

154 (211)
King Unas is the source of food

by the King

To say the words :

'My detestation is hunger,
and I, King Unas will never eat it !
My detestation is thirst,
and I will never drink it !

It is indeed I who will give bread to those who exist, for my foster-mother is the milk-goddess, and she will make it possible for me to live. It is indeed she who bore me.

I was conceived in the night.
I was born in the night.
I belong to the Followers of Re,
who are before the Morning Star.
I was conceived in Nun. I was born in Nun.
I have come and I have brought to You
the bread of those I found there !'

155 (212)
King Unas eats and drinks what Horus lives on

by the King

To say the words :

'The Eye of Horus drips on the bush of the Denu-plant and Foremost of the Westerners came for it, having fetched provisions to Horus, foremost of the houses.

What he (Horus) lives on,
I, King Unas live on !
What he eats of, I eat of !
What he drinks of,
I drink of !
A joint of roast meat,
that is my offering !

Passageway
Towards the Horizon

Offerings of Offerings : Water, Fire, Kas
Passageway - North Wall

156 (199)
reversion of offerings

by the priest

'O Osiris King Unas,
[turn yourself to this your bread, accept it from me.]'

To say the words four times :
'May the Eye of Horus endure [with You.]'
[*-the reversion] of divine offering-*

157 (32)
pouring of libation under the feet

by the priest

'This is your libation, Osiris.
This is your libation,
O King Unas,
have gone forth *-libation & two pellets of natron-*
to your son,
have gone forth to Horus.

I have come and I bring You the Eye of Horus, that your heart may be refreshed with it. I bring it to You under your feet. Take the outflow that comes out from You. Your heart will not be weary with it.'

To say the words four times :

'Come, (for) You have been invoked !'

158 (23)
purification by water

by the priest

'Osiris, seize all those who hate King Unas -*pour water*- and who speak evil against his name. Thoth, go, seize him for Osiris. Bring him who speaks evil against the name of King Unas. Put him in your hand.'

To say the words four times :

'Do not let go of him ! Beware, do not let go of him !'
-*pour water*-

159 (25)
censing Ka-rite

by the priest

'Someone has gone with his Ka.
Horus has gone with his Ka.
Seth has gone with his Ka.
Thoth has gone with his Ka.

O King Unas,
the arm of your Ka is before You !
O King Unas,
the arm of your Ka is behind You !
O King Unas,
the foot of your Ka is before You !
O King Unas,
the foot of your Ka is behind You !

O Osiris King Unas,
I have given You the Eye of Horus !
May your face be adorned with it !
May the perfume of the Eye of Horus diffuse over You !'

160 (200)
glorification of incense as the Eye of Horus

by the priest

'Salutations to You, incense !
Salutations to You, brother of the god !
Salutations to You,
Great So-and-so in the limbs of Horus !

You of great purity, spread yourself in your identity of the cake (of incense) : let your scent be on King Unas and purify King Unas.

O Eye of Horu,
be high and great toward King Unas !'
-*incense*-

> Towards the threshold of the Akhet
> Passageway - South Wall

161 (244)
smashing the vessels of offering

by the priest

'This is the [firm] Eye of [Horus] !
It has been set for You that You may become strong and he may become afraid of You !'
-*smashing the redware*-

162 (245)
the King is a star escaping Osiris

by the King

'I, King Unas, have come to You, O Nut ! I have come to You, O Nut, having left my father on Earth, having left

Horus behind me, having grown wings as a falcon, feathered as a hawk, my Ba having fetched him, his magic having equipped me.'

by Nut

'(O King Unas), You shall split open your place in the sky among the stars of the sky, for You are the Lone Star, the companion of Hu.

May You look down upon the head of Osiris as he governs the Akhs, while You yourself stand far from him. You are not of them and You will not be of them !'

163 (246)
standing at the door of the horizon

by the priest

'This King Unas stance as a ram with two wild-bull horns on his head has been seen. For You are a black ram, (King Unas), the son of a black ewe, whom a white ewe bore and four teats suckled.

Blue-eyed Horus has come against You (gods) : beware of red-eyed Horus ! The one with painful wrath - his Ba cannot be barred !

His messengers have gone, his couriers have run, and they bear tidings to the One with sweeping shoulders in the East : "The one of yours has gone, of whom the god says that he will govern the gods' fathers.

The gods shall grow silent for You, the Ennead having put their hands to their mouth, before this one of yours, of whom the god says that he will govern the gods' fathers."

Stand at the doors of the horizon, (King Unas), open the doors of the Cool Waters, and stand at the head, like

Geb at the fore of his Ennead.

They go in, they will smite down evil. They come out, they will lift up their face and see You as Min at the head of the Two Shrines.

Someone has stood up behind You, (Re) : your brother has stood up behind You, the one You summoned has stood up behind You. You will not perish, (King Unas) !

You will not cease ! Your name will <endure> among men, even as your name comes to be with the gods !'

the Ankh
sacred glyph of life

The Antechamber
The Akhet

Osiris King Unas is Solar
West Gable

Osiris King emerges from the Duat

164 (247)
Osiris king Unas awakened by Horus

by the priest

To say the words :

'Your son Horus has done this for You !

The Great Ones will tremble,
having seen the knife which is in your hand,
when You ascend from the Duat !
Greetings to You, O Wise One !
Geb has created You !
The Ennead has borne You !
Horus has become pleased with his father !
Atum has become pleased with his years !

The gods of East and West have become pleased with the great thing which came into being in his embrace : the birth of the god !'

by Horus

'O King Unas, O King Unas, see !
O King Unas, O King Unas, look !
O King Unas, O King Unas, hear !
O King Unas, O King Unas, be (there) !
O King Unas, O King Unas,
raise yourself from your side !

So do as I command !
You who hate sleep, but who were made limp.

Arise, You in Nedit !
Your good bread has been prepared in Pe !
Take your control of Heliopolis !

It is Horus (who speaks),
having been commanded to help his father.
As for the Lord of Storm,
the one with spittle near him, Seth, he will bear You :
he is the one who will bear Atum !'

The Solar Destiny of the King

165 (248)
King Unas' stellar destiny revealed

by the priest

To say the words :

'King Unas is a Great One !
King Unas has come out
between the thighs of the Ennead.

King Unas was conceived by Sekhmet, and Shezmetet
bore the King, a star with a sharp front and far travelling,
who brings what the above has for Re daily.

King Unas has come to his throne
with the Two Ladies on it.
King Unas has appeared as a star.'

166 (249)
the Living Horus as Nefertem

by the King

To say the words :

'O You two fighters, tell the Noble One, whoever he may be, that I, King Unas, am this water-lily which sprang up clean from the Earth.

I have been received
by him who prepared my throne.

I am at the nose of the controlling power.
I have come from the Island of Fire.
I have set Ma'at in it in the place of disorder.

I am on my way to the linen garments which the Uraei guard on the night of the great flood which came forth from the great goddess.

I appear as Nefertem, as the water-lily at the nose of Re, as he emerges from the horizon daily, the one at the sight of whom the gods become cleansed !'

167 (250)
the King as understanding and wisdom

by the priest

To say the words :

'This is King Unas who is in charge of Kas, who unites hearts for the Great One in charge of wisdom, the one who bears the divine scroll - Sia, at the West of Re.'

by the King

'I, King Unas, have come to my throne which is in charge of Kas. I will join minds, You in charge of wisdom, (being) great ! I will become Sia who bears the divine scroll, who is at the West of Re, tended by my hand. I say what is on the mind of the Great One on the Festival of the Red Linen.

That is King Unas, I am Sia who is at the West of Re, <reserved> of heart, at the fore of the Cavern of Nun.'

Final goodbye to the Duat

168 (251)
King's address to stars and gods of the Duat

by the King

To say the words :

'O You who are in charge of the hours, who precede Re, make way for me so that I, King Unas, may pass within the Circuit of Warlike-Face.

I am off to this throne of mine, foremost of thrones, (as) one who is behind the <great> god, with a set head adorned with a sharp strong antelope horn, as one who carries a sharp knife which cuts throats, (a horn) that removes strife from the head of the bull and makes those in darkness quiver, a strong horn behind the great god.

I have subdued those who were caught, I have smitten their heart. My arm cannot be opposed in the horizon.'

The King merges with Re

169 (252)
the King united with Re

by the priest

To say the words :

'Lift up your face,
You gods in the Duat,
for King Unas has come

that You might see him
changed into the great god.
King Unas is ushered in trembling.
King Unas is robed as Lord of You All !
King Unas will govern the people.
King Unas will judge the living within the shore of Re.
King Unas will speak with Him who judged between the
two gods at the clean shore
in which he has made his dwelling.
King Unas has (the icon of) power on his head.
King Unas wields the Ames-staff
and it causes respect for King Unas.
King Unas will sit with the rower of the Bark of Re.
When King Unas commands what is good,
he will do it.
King Unas is the great god.'

The Duat purified the King

170 (253)
the title of the King lifted up by Shu

by the priest

To say the words :

'Someone has become clean
in the Field of Reeds !
Re has become clean
in the Field of Reeds !
Someone has become clean
in the Field of Reeds !
This King Unas has become clean
in the Field of Reeds.
The title of this King Unas
is given by Re.
O Nut, take his title !
O Shu, lift it up !
O Shu, lift it up !'

The Horus-King acquires the Horizon
West Wall

The King as Horus of the South (Hierakonpolis)

171 (254)
Horus the King at the entrance of the horizon

by the priest

'The Great One will be censed for the Bull of Nekhen,
and the flame of the blast will be toward You
who are around the shrine.'

by the King

'O great god whose name is unknown !
A meal in place for the Sole Lord !
O Lord of the Horizon,
make ready a place for me, King Unas !
For if You fail to make ready a place for me,
I will lay a curse on my father Geb, (saying) :

"The Earth will speak no more.
Geb has no <guard>."

Whoever I find in my way, I will devour.
The pelican will prophesy !
The Sunshine bird will go up !
The Great One will arise !'

The Enneads will speak (saying) :

'The Earth being entirely dammed up, for the mountain ranges on either side of the river have been joined together and the riverbanks have been united, the roads have been made impassable to travellers, and the slopes have been destroyed for those who would go up.'
By the god with the great plow :

'The rope has been guided, the <beaten path> crossed and the ball struck at the mouth of the Apis's canal.

Oho ! Your fields are in fear, You Climbing Star, before the Pillar of the Stars, for they have seen the Pillar of Kenzet, the Bull of the Sky, and the Oxherd shall be overwhelmed upon its stem.

Oho ! Fear and trembling shall descend upon the Knife-Bearers before the storm of the sky, for he has parted the Earth by means of what he knew, on the day when he wished to come - so says the god with the great plow who is in the midst of the Duat.'

By the Beautiful West :

'See, she comes to meet You,
the goddess of the Beautiful West,
meeting You with her lovely tresses !

She says :

"Here comes he whom I gave birth, whose horn is upstanding, eye-painted pillar, the Bull of the Sky ! Your shape is notable !

Pass in peace, for I have protected You." - so says the Beautiful West to King Unas.'

by Thighs-Forward :

'"Go, row to the Field of Offerings and travel to Him who is on his high tree.", so says Thighs-Forward. "You plow into the Earth to your thickness, to your middle, to your shoulders. You shall see Re in his fetters, You shall praise Re in his loosing from fetters by means of the aegis of the Great One, which is in its red linen. The Lord of Peace is giving You your [title]."'

by the King :

'O You apes who cut off heads, I, King Unas, will pass by You in peace, for I have tied my head to my neck, and my neck is on my torso in this my name of Head-Tier, by means of which I tied the head of Apis on that day when the longhorned bull was lassoed.

Since I have allowed them <to eat> from their cups and drink from their inundation, so shall I be protected in the same by those who see me.

The jubilation uraeus, Tefnut of King Unas, who supports Shu, is on her electrum staff, widening my place in Busiris, in Mendes and in Djedut, erecting dual standards in front of the Great Ones, excavating a pool for me in the Field of Reeds, and confirming my farmland in the Field of Offerings.

I will give judgment between the two contestants in the Great Immersion, for my power is the power of the Eye of Tebi, my strength is the strength of the Eye of Tebi.

I have protected myself from those who would do this against me, who would take away my food from me, who, when it was there, would take my supper from me and who, when it was there, would take the breath from my nose and who would bring to an end my days of life.

My force will be against them, when he is apparent on my shore. Their hearts will fall to my fingers, their entrails are for the denizens of the sky, their red parts are for the denizens of the Earth ! Their heirs are to be poor, their houses to conflagration, and their courtyards to the high Nile ! But my heart is sweet, my heart is sweet, for I am the unique one, the Bull of the Sky, for I have crushed those who would do this against me and have annihilated their survivors.

That which appertains to my throne, (that) which I have taken and lifted up, is this which my father Shu gave me in the presence of Seth.'

172 (255)
the King subdues the Hateful One

by the priest

To say the words :

'The horizon will be censed for Horus of Nekhen.
A meal for the Lords !
The horizon will be censed for Horus of Nekhen.
The flame of <its> blast will be <toward You>
who are around the shrine !
The outburst of its blast will be toward You
who raise up the Great One !
The horizon will be censed for Horus of Nekhen.
A meal for the Lords !'

by the King

'[O You Hateful One], hateful of character and hateful of shape, remove yourself from your place and lay your insignia of rank on the ground for me. If You do not remove yourself from your place [and lay your insignia of rank on the ground] for me, then I, King Unas, will come, my face being that of this Great One, the Lord of Power who is strong through the injury which was done to him. I will put [flame in my Eye], and it will encompass You and set storm among the doers of (evil) deeds, gushing its (fiery) outburst among these primeval ones. I will smite away [the arms of Shu which support the sky] and I will thrust my shoulder into that rampart on which You lean.

The Great One indeed will rise within his shrine
[and lay his insignia on the ground for] me,

for I have assumed authorative speech and have power through understanding.'

173 (256)
the King on the throne of Horus

by the King

To say the words :

'I, King Unas, have succeeded to Geb !
I have succeeded to Geb !
I have succeeded to Atum !
I am on the throne of Horus the first-born !
His Eye is my strength ! I am protected from what was done against him.

The flaming blast of my Uraeus is that of Renenutet on my head. I have set the fear of me in their hearts by making strife with them. I have seen the gods naked and bowing to me in adoration.

Row me, O mother of mine !
Tow me, O abode of mine ! Haul your cable !'

174 (257)
the King breaks through the sky-canopy

by the priest

To say the words :

'There is excitement in the sky :
"We saw something new !", say the primeval gods.
O You Ennead, Horus is in the Sunlight !
Let the Lords of Forms terrorize for him.
Let Atum's Dual Ennead serve him as he sits on the throne of the Lord of All.
King Unas will acquire the sky,
and cleave its iron.

King Unas will lead <on> the roads to Kheprer.
When King Unas rests in life in the West,
those of the Duat attend him.
When King Unas shines anew in the East,
he who settled the dispute
will come to him bowing.
The gods will terrorize for King Unas,
since he is older than the Great One
and belongs to the control of his throne.
King Unas will assume authorative speech.
Eternity shall be brought to him.
Understanding shall be placed
for him at his feet.
Haul (the sky-boat) for King Unas,
for he has acquired the horizon.'

The King as a Living Osiris

175 (258)
the Horus King is Osiris headed to Re's sky

by the priest

To say the words :

'King Unas is Osiris in a dust-devil. Earth is his detestation !

King Unas will not enter into Geb, lest his bones perish and lest he sleeps in his mansion upon Earth ; his bones are [made strong], his ills are removed. King Unas has become pure through the Eye of Horus. His ill has been removed by the two Kites of Osiris. King Unas has shed his outflow to Earth in Qus.

It is his sister (Wadjet), the Lady of Pe,
who laments him, (saying) : "King Unas goes to the
sky ! King Unas goes to the sky !
On the wind ! On the wind !"

He shall not be turned away, and there is none who will turn away from him. He shall not sit in the tribunal of the god."

King Unas is the one who is <on his own>, the eldest of the gods : his bread-offering is for above with Re, his feast is from Nun !

King Unas is the one who goes to and fro, coming and going with Re and embracing his mansions.

King Unas will bestow Kas and take away Kas. He will impose an obstacle and remove an obstacle.

King Unas will spend day and night appeasing the Two Adzes (Horus and Seth) in Hermopolis. His foot will not be opposed, his heart cannot be barred.'

The King is a Living Horus

176 (260)
Living Horus vindicated by the Two Truths

by the King

To say the words :

'O Geb ! Bull of Nut ! I, King Unas, am Horus, the heir of my father. I have gone and came back, the fourth of these four gods who have brought water, who have administered purification,

> On the Way to the Sky of Re
> South Wall

176 (260)
Living Horus vindicated by the Two Truths
(West Wall continues on South Wall)

who have rejoiced in the strength of their fathers, one who desires to be vindicated by what he has done.

For judgment between the orphan and the orphaness has been made for me. The Two Truths have heard (the case), while Shu was witness and the Two Truths commanded that the thrones of Geb revert to me, so that I raise myself to what I have desired, my limbs - which were in concealment- join, I unite those who are in Nun and put a stop to the affair in Heliopolis.

Now that I go forth today in the real form of a living Akh, I shall break up the fight and punish strife. I have come forth for Ma'at, (so) that I may bring her, she being with me. Wrath will depart for me and those who are in Nun will assign life to me.

My refuge is my Eye !
My protection is <my> Eye !
My strength is my Eye !
My power is my Eye !

O You southern, northern, western, and eastern gods, honour me and fear me, for I sat down in the <pavilion> of the dual courtyards. That effective uraeus Djenenutet will burn for You, and strike your hearts.

O You who would come against me in obstruction, come to me, come to me !

I am the very person of my father,
the bud of my mother.
I detest travelling in darkness,
for then I cannot see those who are upside down.

I go forth today that I may bring Ma'at,
for she is with me.

I will not be given to your flame,
O You gods.'

177 (261)
the King is a Lightning Flash

by the priest

To say the words :

'King Unas is woe to the heart, the son of the heart of Shu, extensively extended and with a terrible brilliance ! King Unas is a flame (burning) before the wind, to the end of the sky and to the end of the Earth, when the hand of the lightning bolts have become empty of King Unas. King Unas will traverse Shu, travel the horizon, and kiss the Red Crown as one hurled by a god. Those who are in <the firmament> will open their arms to him.

King Unas will stand up on the eastern side of the quartz of rain, and there is brought to him a way of ascent to the sky. It is he who does the mission of the Stormy One (Seth).'

The Horus-king in the afterlife

178 (262)
the King reminds the deities he knows them

by the King

To say the words :

'Be not unaware of me, O god, since You know me,
I know You. And I know You !
Be not unaware of me, O Re.
Know me, for I know You.
Be not unaware of me, O Re.
I call You : "Great of Provision, Lord of All !"
Be not unaware of me, O Thoth.
Know me, for I know You.
Be not unaware of me, O Thoth.;

I call You : "He Who Sets Alone !"
Be not unaware of me, O Sharp Horus.
Know me, for I know You.

Be not unaware of me, O Sharp Horus.
Know me, for I know You.
I call You : "The Difficult One !"

Be not unaware of me, O Dweller in the Duat.
Know me, for I know You.

Be not unaware of me, O Dweller in the Duat.
I call You : "He Who Wakes Sound !"

Be not unaware of me, Sky Bull.
Know me, for I know You.
Be not unaware of me, O Bull of the Sky.
I call You : "This One Who Endures !"

Behold, I have come !
Behold, I have come !
Behold, I have emerged !

I have not come of my own accord, a message having come for me. I have passed by my House of my Ba, the striking power of the Great Lake has missed me. There is no one who requires my fare for the great ferry.

There is no one who bars me from the White Palace of the Great Ones at the Beaten Path of Stars - for look, I have reached the height of heaven.

I have seen the cobra in the Nightboat, and it is I who row in it. I have recognized the uraeus in the Dayboat, and it is I who bail it out. The Sun-folk have testified concerning me. The hailstorms of the sky have taken me (so) that they might raise me up to Re.'

179 (263)
the spirits of the dead meet the King

by the King

To say the words :

'The two reed floats of the sky have been set in place for Re, that he might cross on them to the horizon. The two reed floats of the sky have been set in place for Horus of the Horizon, that Horus of the Horizon might cross on them to Re.

The two reed floats of the sky have been set in place for me, that I, King Unas, might cross on them to the horizon, to Re. The two reed floats of the sky have been set in place for me, that I might cross on them to Horus of the Horizon and to Re.

It has become well with me and my Ka !
I will live with my Ka !
My panther-skin is on me.
My Ames-staff is on my arm.
My Aba-scepter is in my hand.

Those who have gone away have missed me. They will bring me these four Akhs, the Elders who are at the head of the wearers of the side-lock, who stand in the eastern side of the sky and who sweep away with their electrum staves, that they may tell my good name to Re and announce me to Kas-Assigner, (saying) :

"Greet this King Unas' entrance into the North of the Field of Reeds. Let King Unas across the Winding Canal. He is ferried over to the eastern side of the horizon ! He is ferried over to the eastern side of the sky !
His sister is Sothis !
His female sibling is the Morning Star !"'

180 (267)
leaving Osiris behind, crossing the horizon

by the King

To say the words :

'You have your heart, O Osiris !
You have your legs, O Osiris !
You have your arms, O Osiris !
(So too) my heart is my own !
My legs are my own !
My arms are my own !

A stairway to the sky is set up for me that I, King Unas, may ascend on it to the sky. I will ascend on the smoke of the great censing. I will fly up as a bird and alight as a beetle. When I will fly up as a bird and alight as a beetle, it will be in the empty throne in your Bark, O Re.

Stand up, remove yourself, O You who do not know the thicket of reeds (of the horizon), that I may sit in your place. I will row in the sky in your Bark, O Re. I will push off from the land in your Bark, O Re.'

When You are emerging from the horizon, I, with my scepter in my arm, will be the one sailing your Bark, O Re, (so) that You may ascend to the sky and (I may) go away from the land, away from wife and kilt.'

181 (268)
the Royal Ka of the King comes to him

by the priest

To say the words :

'This King Unas will wash himself when Re appears and the Elder Ennead shines. Should he of Ombos become high at the head of the conclave, (then) this King Unas will take over the nobles as a limb of himself, and this King Unas will seize hold of the Great White Crown from the hands of the Two Enneads. Isis [will nurse him. Nephthys will suckle him.] Horus [will accept him] beside him at his two fingers, purify this King Unas in the Jackal Lake, and release the Ka of this King Unas in the Lake of the Duat. He will purge the flesh of the Ka of this King Unas and of his body by means of that which is on the shoulders of Re in the horizon, which he receives when the Two Lands shine and he opens the faces of the gods. He will conduct the Ka of this King Unas to his body at the Great Mansion.

The portals will act for him, the Curl (of the Red Crown) will be tied on for him and this King Unas will guide the Imperishable Stars ! He will ferry across to the Fields of Reeds with those who are in the horizon rowing him and those who are in the firmament sailing him.

This King Unas will become truly efficient, and his arms will not fail. This King Unas will become truly excellent, and his Ka will reach him !'

182 (269)
censing prayer, ascension and sweet milk

by the King

To say the words :

'The fire is laid, the fire shines.
The incense is laid on the fire, the incense shines.
Your scent has come to me, O incense,
may my scent come to You, O incense.
Your scent has come to me, You gods,
may my scent come to You, You gods.
I, King Unas, shall be with You, gods ;
You shall be with me, gods.
I, King Unas, live with You, gods ;

You shall live with me, gods.
I, King Unas,
shall love You, gods ;
love me, gods.

ascension

The wafer has come, the cap that comes from the knee of Horus has come : the ascender has come, the ascender has come ; the climber has come, the climber has come ; he who flew up has come, he who flew up has come ! I will ascend upon the thighs of Isis ! I will climb up upon the thighs of Nephthys ! My father Atum will seize my hand for me, and allot me to those excellent and wise gods : the Imperishable Stars !

sweet milk

My mother Ipy, give me that breast of yours, that I may apply it to my mouth and suck this white, gleaming, sweet milk of yours. As for yonder land in which I walk, I will neither thirst nor hunger in it, forever !'

183 (270)
summoning Osiris as ferryman

by the priest

To say the words :

'Awake in peace !

Face Behind Him, in peace !
Sees Behind Him, in peace !

Ferryman of the sky, in peace !
Ferryman of Nut, in peace !
Ferryman of the gods, in peace !'

by the King

'I have come to You that You may ferry me across in this ferryboat in which You ferry the gods. I have come to his side, just like a god coming to his side.

I have come near to his side,
just like a god coming near to his side.
There is no one living
who makes accusation against me.
There is no one dead
who makes accusation against me.
There is no duck which makes accusation against me.
There is no longhorned bull
which makes accusation against me.
So, if You should not ferry me over, I will leap up and put myself on the wing of Thoth, and he will ferry me over to yonder side.'

184 (271)
raising the Djed-Pillar

by the King

To say the words :

'I, King Unas,
have inundated the land
that came forth from the lake.
I have torn out the papyrus-plant.
It is I, (who) satisfied, (the) Two Lands.
It is I, (who) united, (the) Two Lands.
It is I, (who) joined my mother, the Great Wild Cow.
O my mother, the Wild Cow on the hill of grass and on the hill of the stork. Stand up, You two Djed-pillars, and descend, You crossbars, that I may ascend on this ladder which my father Re made for me.

Horus and Seth shall take hold of my arm and take me away from the Duat. You with the eye-injury, beware of him with the command ; You with the command, beware of him with the eye-injury.

The face of the god is open to me, and I sit on the great throne beside the god.'

185 (272)
opening the Gate of Nun

by the King

To say the words :

'O Height that will not be penetrated, Gate of Nun, I, King Unas, have come to You, have this opened to me !'

by the gate :

'Is King Unas the little one in it ?'

by the King

'I am at the head of the Followers of Re !
I am not at the head of the gods
who make disturbance !'

King Unas

The Book of Ascension
North Wall

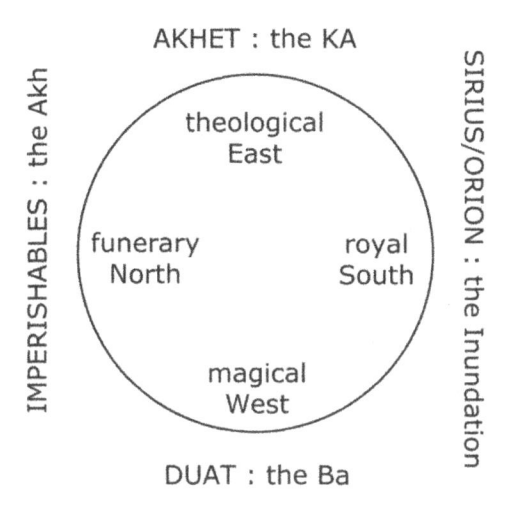

AKHET : the KA

IMPERISHABLES : the Akh

theological East

funerary North

royal South

magical West

SIRIUS/ORION : the Inundation

DUAT : the Ba

the semantic structure of the tomb

King Unas flies away, ferries over and climbs ladders

186 (302)
the King flies away to Re

by the King

To say the words :

'The sky has been bled (at dawn) and Sothis lives, because I, King Unas, I am a living one, the son of Sothis, for whom the Dual Ennead have cleaned the imperishable Striker. My house in the sky will not end. My throne of the Two Lands on Earth will not end.

Men hide,
(but) the gods fly away !

Sothis has flown me to the sky into the company of my brothers the gods. Nut the great has uncovered her arms for me. The Two Bas, who are at the head of the Bas of Iunu (Heliopolis), who attend on Re, have bowed themselves, they who spend the night making this mourning for the god.

My seat is with You, O Re, and I will give it to nobody else. I will ascend to the sky to You, O Re, for my face is that of falcons, my wings are those of birds, my talons are the fangs of Him of Atfet.

There is no word against me on Earth among men, there is no accusation in the sky among the gods. For I annulled the word against me, which I destroyed in order to mount up to the sky.

Paths-Parter (Wepwawet) has flown me up to the sky among my brethren the gods.

I use my arms as a Nile goose,
I flap my wings as a kite.

The flier has flown !

O men,
I have flown away from You !'

187 (303)
the King ferries over to the sky

by the King

To say the words :

'O western gods, eastern gods, southern gods, and northern gods ! These four pure reed-floats which You set down for Osiris when he ascended to the sky, so that he might ferry over to the Cool Waters with his son Horus at his fingers, so that he might foster him and cause him to appear as a great god in the Cool Waters - set them down for me, King Unas !'

by the gods :

'Are You Horus,
son of Osiris ?
Are You, King Unas,
the god, the eldest one, the son of Hathor ?

Are You the seed of Geb ?'

by the King

'Osiris has commanded me, King Unas, to appear as the counterpart of Horus, and these four Akhs who are in Heliopolis have written (it) on the record of the two great gods who are in the Cool Waters.'

188 (304)
a ladder in the necropolis

by the King

To say the words :

'Hail to You, daughter of Anubis, who is at the windows of the sky, the companion of Thoth, who is at the uprights of the ladder ! Open my way that I, King Unas, may pass.

Greetings to You, ostrich at the lips of the Winding Canal ! Open my way that I may pass !

Greetings, Bull of Re who has four horns : a horn of yours in the West, a horn of yours in the East, a horn of yours in the South, and a horn of yours in the North ! Bend down for me this western horn of yours, (so) that I may pass.'

by the Bull of Re :

'Are You a pure Westerner,
for You have come forth from Falcon City ?'

by the King

'Greetings to You, Field of Peace !
Greetings to the vegetation [that is in You !
Greetings to] my vegetation that is in You,
the clean growth therein is pleasant !'

189 (305)
a Ladder is made for the King

by the King

To say the words :

'A ladder has been is knotted together by Re, face to face with Osiris. A ladder has been knotted together by Horus, face to face with his father Osiris when he goes to his Akh, one of them being on this side, one of them being on that side, while I, King Unas, am between them.'

by the gods :

'Are You a god whose places are pure ?'

by the King

'I have come forth from a pure (place).'
'Stand up, King Unas !', says Horus.

by Seth :

'Sit down, King Unas !', says Seth.
'Take his arm !', says Re.'

by the priest

'Akh, to the sky !
Corpse, to the Earth !

What people receive when they are buried, their thousand of bread and their thousand of beer, is from the offering table of the Foremost of the Westerners.

Poor is the heir who has no writing.
So King Unas writes with his big finger
and does not write with his little finger.'

190 (306)
the King mounts up the Ladder

by the priest

To say the words :

'"How lovely to see ! How pleasing to behold," say they, namely the gods, when you ascend to the sky with your power upon you, your terror about you, and your magic at your feet.

Geb has acted on your behalf just in the manner in which things should be done for you.

There have come to You the divine Bas of Pe, the divine Bas of Nekhen, the gods who belong to the sky, and the gods who belong to the Earth, (so) that they might make support for You, upon their arms.

So, ascend, King Unas, to the sky and mount up on it in this its identity of "Ladder".

"The sky will be given to King Unas, and the Earth will be given to him.", says Atum.

It is Geb who is the one who argues for it, (saying) :

"The mounds praised are the Mounds of Horus and the Mounds of Seth, and the Fields of Reeds shall adore You in this your name of Morning God, as Sobek under his mangroves."

Has he (Seth) slain You, his heart having said that You would die because of him ? But look, You have become a more Enduring Bull of the Wild Bulls than he !

Endure, endure, O Enduring Bull,
(so) that You, King Unas, may be enduring
at the head of them,
at the head of the Akhs forever !'

Except for Re, King Unas rules all.

191 (307)
the King is the Bull of Heliopolis

by the King

To say the words :

'There is a Heliopolitan in me, O god !
Your Heliopolitan (nature) is in me, O god !
There is a Heliopolitan in me, O Re !
Your Heliopolitan (nature) is in me, O Re !
My mother is a Heliopolitan,
my father is a Heliopolitan.

I, King Unas, am a Heliopolitan myself, born in Heliopolis when Re was ruler of the Dual Ennead and above the plebs, Nefertem without peer, heir of my father Geb.

As for any god who will thrust out his arm (to hold me off), when my face turns to worship You and to call to You about my body, O god, and about my nose, O god,

he will have no bread ;
he will have no wafer
in the company of his brothers the gods ;
he will not send (messengers) ;
he will not leap <the barrier>
in the company of his brothers the gods ;
the doors of the Nightboat will not be opened to him ;
the doors of the Dayboat will not be opened to him ;
he will not be judged as a citizen ;
the doors of provisioning will not be opened to him !

I have come for You !
For I am the Wild Bull of the savannah, the Great-faced Bull who comes from Heliopolis.

I am both the one who gave You birth and the one who can continue to give You birth.'

192 (308)
the gods invoke the King naked

by the King

To say the words :

'Greetings to You,
Horus on the Mounds of Horus !
Greetings to You, Seth on the Mounds of Seth !
Greetings to You, Reeds in the Field of Reeds !
Greetings, You two reconciled gods, twin children of
the four foremost gods of the Great Mansion,
You who invoke me naked !
I, King Unas,
have looked on You as Horus looked at Isis.
I have looked at You
as Ka-Assigner looked on Serket.
I have looked at You
as Sobek looked at Neith.
I have looked at You
as Seth looked at the two reconciled (gods).'

193 (309)
the King is the servant of Re

by the King

To say the words :

'I, King Unas,
I am <the accountant> of the god,
in charge of the Mansion of Re,
born of Prayer-of-the-gods,
who is in the prow of the Boat of Re.
I shall sit before him,
I shall open his boxes,
I shall break open his edicts,
I shall seal his dispatches,
I shall send out his unwearying messengers,
and I shall do what he says to me.'

194 (310)
the King warns the gods

by the King

To say the words :

'If I, King Unas, should be cursed,
then will Atum be cursed.
If I should be reviled,
then will Atum be reviled.
If I should be smitten,
then will Atum be smitten.
If I should be hindered on this road,
then will Atum be hindered.
I am Horus !
I have come in the wake of my father !
I have come in the wake of Osiris !
O You (ferryman), who faces forward and backward,
bring this (ferryboat) to me !'

by the ferryman :

'Which ferryboat should I get for You ?'

by the King

Bring me : 'Whenever It Flies It Lands !'

195 (311)
the King wants to be seen by Re and sees Re

by the King

To say the words :

'See me, O Re !
Recognize me, O Re !

I, King Unas,
belong to those that know You, so know me.

I will not forget the blessing of the given offering, (so that) she who maroons whom she would maroon will open the doors of the horizon at the ascent of the Dayboat. I know the Hall of the Baldachin in the middle of the Platform of Izken from which You go forth when You board the Nightboat.

Commend me, commend me,
commend me,

-to say the words four times without pause-

to those four of yours who go down behind You, and who see with two faces and who argue with fierce <roaring> about the first-born with those who will have trouble, along with those whom they would destroy, (so that) they will not cross (him with) their arm when I turn to You, when I come to You and tell You this name of yours of "Great Flood which came forth from the Great One".

I will not become blind if You put me in darkness. I will not become deaf even though I do not hear your voice.

You should take me with You, with You !

He who will drive away storms for You, who will dispel the clouds for You, and who will break up the hail for You. I will make genuflection after genuflection for You ! I will make adoration after adoration for You when You set me on the body of the vulture !'

196 (312)
the King as ascending bread

by the King

To say the words :

'The bread has flown !
The bread has indeed flown, toward my mansions, the Mansions of the Red Crown !'

Cannibal Hymn (fragment)

Arrival in Heaven
East Gable

197 (273-274)
the Cannibal Hymn

by the priest

'The sky rains down.
The stars darken.
The celestial vaults stagger.
The bones of Aker tremble.

The <decans> are stilled against them, at seeing King Unas rise as a Ba. A god who lives on his fathers and feeds on his mothers.

King Unas is Lord of Wisdom
whose mother knows not his name.
The glory of King Unas is in the sky,
his might is in the horizon.
Like his father, Atum, his begetter.
Though his son, King Unas is mightier than he.

The Kas of King Unas are behind him.
His guardian forces are under his feet.
His gods are over him.
His Uraeus-serpents are on his brow.
The guiding-serpent of King Unas is on his forehead :
she who sees the Ba (of the enemy as)
good for <burning>.
The neck of King Unas is on his trunk.

King Unas is the Bull of the Sky,
who <shatters> at will,
who lives on the being of every god,
who eats their <entrails>,
even of those who come with their bodies
full of magic from the Island of Fire.

King Unas is one equipped,
who assembles his Akhs.
King Unas appears as this Great One,
Lord of those with (Helping) Hands.
He sits with his back to Geb,
for it is King Unas who weighs what he says,
together with Him-whose-name-is-hidden,
on this day of slaying the oldest ones.

King Unas is Lord of Offerings,
who knots the cord,
and who himself prepares his meal.

King Unas is he who eats men and lives on gods, Lord of Porters, who dispatches written messages.

It is "Grasper-of-the-top-knot", <who is> Kehau, who lassoes them for King Unas.

It is "Serpent Raised-head", who guards them for him and restrains them for him. It is "He-upon-the-willows", who binds them for him.

It is Courser, slayer of Lords, who will cut their throats for King Unas, and will extract for him what is in their bodies, for he is the messenger whom King Unas sends to restrain.

It is Shezmu, who will cut them up for King Unas, and cooks meals of them in his dinner-pots.

(274)

It is King Unas who eats their magic and gulps down their Akhs.

Their big ones are for his morning meal, their middle-sized ones are for his evening meal, their little ones are for his night meal, their old men and their old women are for his incense-burning.

It is the Great Ones in the North of the sky, who light the fire for him, to the cauldrons containing them, with the thighs of their eldest (as fuel).

Those who are in the sky serve King Unas, and the butcher's blocks are wiped over for him, with the feet of their women.

He has revolved around the whole of the two skies. He has circled the two banks.

For King Unas is the great power that overpowers the powers. King Unas is a sacred image, the most sacred image of the sacred images of the Great One.

Whom he finds in his way, him he devours <bit by bit>.

The place of King Unas is at the head of all the noble ones who are in the horizon.

For King Unas is a god, older than the oldest.

Thousands revolve around him, hundreds offer to him. There is given to him a warrant as a great power by Orion, the father of the gods.

King Unas has risen again in the sky.
He is crowned as Lord of the Horizon.
He has smashed the back-bones,
and has seized the hearts of the gods.
He has eaten the Red Crown.
He has swallowed the Green One.
King Unas feeds on the lungs of the wise.
And likes to live on hearts and their magic.

King Unas abhors against licking
<the Coils of the Red Crown>.
But delights to have their magic in his belly.

The dignities of King Unas
will not be taken away from him.

For he has swallowed
the knowledge of every god.

The lifetime of King Unas is eternal repetition.
His limit is everlastingness.

In this his dignity of : "If-he-likes-he-does.
If-he-dislikes-he-does-not."

He who is at the limits of the horizon,
forever and ever.

Lo, their Ba is in the belly of King Unas.

Their Akhs are in the possession of King Unas, as the surplus of his meal <out of> the gods. Which is cooked for King Unas from their bones.

Lo, their Ba is in the possession of King Unas. Their shadows are removed from their owners, while King Unas is this one who ever rises and lasting lasts.

The doers of ill deeds have no power to destroy, the chosen seat of King Unas, among the living in this land.

Forever and ever.'

198 (275)
opening the double doors of the horizon

by the priest

To say the words :

'King Unas has come to You, falcons, for your Horus-mansions become peaceful to King Unas, with his bent tail, of the intestine of baboon, at his rear.

King Unas will open the double doors.
King Unas will attain the limit of the horizon.
King Unas has laid down his tailed kilt there.
King Unas will become the Great One
who is in Crocodilopolis.'

Protection of the East of the Tomb

199 (276)

by the priest

To say the words :

'Do against yourself what You can do against yourself, You Zekzek-snake who are in your <hole>, You Hindrance !'

Protecting the East
(continuing on the East Wall)

200 (277)

by the priest

[*To say the words* :]

'Horus has fallen because of his Eye !
The Bull has crawled away because of his testicles.
Fall down ! Crawl away !'

201 (278)

by the priest

To say the words :

'Babi has stood up to meet the Foremost of Letepolis :
let the spittle stop the one whose trampling is desired,
You whose trampling is desired.

You are released, Wefi-snake :
cause King Unas to be protected.'

202 (279)

by the priest

To say the words :

'King Unas is a trampler,
who <chops> the mud of the canals.
Thoth, behind King Unas !
Trample on the one of the dark,
trample on the one of the dark !'

203 (280 - 281)

by the priest

To say the words :

'O You Evil-doer, Evil-doer !
O You of the wall, You of the wall !
Set your face behind You !
Beware of the great mouth !
Caught one of the courtyard, You !
Earthen one of the courtyard,
long one, You of the foot,
lion of Pehty, lion of Petjety !
Pehty and Petjety, give me now your long one !
Stack up the flesh.
Woe, now : the pot !

The plaited serpent,
the plaited serpent,
will be conveyed away,
will be conveyed away.'

204 (282)

by the priest

To say the words :

'O Hazet-snake, the vulture's mouth - that is your arrack. Hazet-snake, the vulture's mouth, the one belonging to the Gold of Jubilation, Apparent in Heat and Jubilation.

This is your Bull,
the strong one
against whom this was done.'

205 (283)

by the King

To say the words :

'Shall I, King Unas, chop this left nail of mine against You and set a blow with it for Min, attacker ?

O You who rob,
do not rob !'

206 (284)

by the King

To say the words :

'The one Atum has bitten has filled my mouth, coiling all up. The centipede has been smitten by Him-of-the-Mansion, and He-of-the-Mansion has been smitten by the centipede : that lion is inside this lion ; the two bulls shall fight inside the ibis.'

207 (285)

by the priest

To say the words :

'Your two drops (of poison)
are off to your two (poison) sacs :
spit them out at <once>, now ! Gory !
Spew out, You with the liquid, with water.
O You of the injured eye, headband of Seshau,
rain, You wretched one !
Cobra, reject !
You windpipe, You of the Het-plant, alum !
The lion is dangerous with (his) water.
Extender, do not extend !
It is the windpipe.'

208 (286)

by the King

To say the words :

'Spray not as a long one of the lakes, you Tjetje-snake of the jars ! The Byblites have crawled off. The lake-long-one's Red Crowns shall bring in the lake-long-one, for I shall raise the Red Crowns and You shall praise my name.'

209 (287)

by the priest

[*To say the words :*]

'You whose mother turned him away !
You whose mother turned him away,
are You not such, are You not such ?
Lion, spit out !'

210 (288)

by the priest

To say the words :

'O Hekj-snake, O Hekret-snake,
go away, head off !
The Eye of King Unas, do not look at him !
You shall not effect your mission with King Unas,
spit out and do not come back !'

211 (289)

by the priest

To say the words :

'The bull has fallen to the Sedjeh-snake and the
Sedjeh-snake has fallen to the bull.
Fall down ! Crawl away !'

212 (290)

by the priest

To say the words :

'Face has fallen on face. Face has seen face.
The black-dappled knife has gone forth
and swallowed for itself and acquired for itself.'

213 (291)

by the priest

To say the words :

'Your jubilation has been removed, You white one of the
<hole>, by the one who emerged as worm. Your own

jubilation has been taken away, You white one of the <hole>, by him who emerged as a worm.'

214 (292)

by the priest

To say the words :

'You are one whom the attacker attacked,
You snake whose attack has missed.
Your aggression is for your aggressor,
You snake whose attack has missed.'

215 (293)

by the King

To say the words :

'Get back, You hidden one !
Hide yourself, do not let me, King Unas, see You !

You should not come to where I am, that I, may not pronounce against You this your name of Traveler, son of (the female) Traveler. The Majesty of the Pelican has fallen in the inundation, turned away, turned away ! Monster, lie down !'

216 (294)

by the King

To say the words :

'I, King Unas, am Horus who came forth from the acacia, who came forth from the acacia, to whom it was commanded : "Beware of the lion !" To whom the command went forth : "Beware of the lion !"

I have come forth from my stoppered jar after having spent the night in my stoppered jar, and I will appear at dawn. I have come forth from my stoppered jar, having spent the night in my stoppered jar, and I will appear at dawn.'

217 (295)

by the King

To say the words :

'Mafdet will leap on the neck of the snake who brings his gift, and again on the neck of the serpent with sweeping head. Which is the one who will remain? It is I, King Unas, who will remain !'

218 (296)

by the King

To say the words :

'Tjetju-snake, where are You going ? Wait for me, King Unas, (for) King Unas is Geb. Hemetj-snake, brother of the Hemetjet-snake, your father Djaamiu has died.'

219 (297)

by the King

'My hand has come upon You, <accursed> snake. The one that comes on You is that of Mafdet, at the fore of the Mansion of Life, striking You on your face, and scratching You on your eyes, so that You fall into your dung and crawl into your urine.

Fall down ! Lie down ! Crawl away, that your mother Nut may see You !'

220 (298)

by the King

To say the words :

'Re will appear, his effective Uraeus upon him, against this snake which came forth from the Earth.

You under my fingers, I, King Unas, shall cut off your head with this knife which is in the hand of her who has the face of Mafdet. He shall draw out those things which are in your mouth, and milk your poison with those four cords that trail behind the sandals of Osiris. Monster, lie down ! Bull, crawl away !'

221 (299)

by the King

To say the words :

'Cobra, to the sky !
Centipede of Horus, to the Earth !
The sandals of Horus are treading
on the Lord of the Mansion, the Bull of the Cavern.
Shunned snake,
I, King Unas, cannot be shunned !
My sycamore is my sycamore.
My refuge is my refuge.
Anyone I find in my way I will devour.'

222 (300)

by the King

To say the words :

'O Kherti of Nezat, and You ferryman of the Ikehet which

Khnum made ! Bring this (ferry) for me, for I, King Unas, am Sokar of Rosetau. I am off to where Sokar, Lord of the Spread Lake, dwells. You two, get those (ferries) that cross the desert.'

223 (301)
address to the primeval deities

by the King

To say the words :

'You have your bread-loaf,
O Nun and Naunet !
You pair of the gods,
who joined the gods with their shadow.

You have your bread-loaf,
O Amun and Amaunet !
You pair of the gods,
who joined the gods with their shadow.

You have your bread-loaf,
O Atum and Double-Lion !

Who yourselves created your two gods and their bodies, that is Shu and Tefenet, who made the gods, who begot the gods and established the gods.

Tell your father that I, King Unas, have given You your bread-loaves, that I have contented You with what is yours, and that You should not hinder me when I cross to him at the horizon.

For I know him and know his name : "eternal" is his name ; "the Eternal, Lord of the Year" is his name. He whose arms are a weapon, Horus-who-is-over-the-stars-of-the-sky, who brings Re to life every day, shall refashion me and bring me to life every day !

I have come to You, O Horus of Shat.
I have come to You, O Horus of Shezmet.
I have come to You, O Horus of the East.

Lo, I have brought to You your great eastern eye from the cavern. Accept it from me and be sound, (receive) its water in it and be sound, its gore in it and be sound, its vapor in it and be sound. Ascend to it and take it in this your name of the shawl of the god. You should mount up to it in this your name of Re. Put it on your brow in this its name of "Brow-unguent". You should redden with it in this its name of "Willow". Gleam with it among the gods in this its name of "Faience". Be joyful by means of it in this its name of "Jubilation oil of Renenutet", for it loves You.

Arise, great reed float, as Paths-Parter (Wepwawet), filled with your Akh and emergent from the horizon ! Take the crown from the great and mighty <foreigners> who preside over Libya as Sobek, Lord of Bakhu. When You travel to your fields and course the interior of your mangroves and your nose smells the sweet savours of Shezmet, You should make my Ka ascend for him beside him, just like that coursing of yours ascends for You.

So, clean me !

So, brighten me bright in this Jackal Lake of yours, (O) Jackal, in which You cleanse the gods - powerful for You and sharp for You !

O Horus, Lord of the Malachite !'

To say the words four times.

'Two green falcons.'

Corridor
Threshold to the Imperishables

The Bold of Babi
West Wall

224 (313)
opening the door to the sky

by the priest

'Draw back, the phallus of Babi. The doors of the sky are opened, the King has opened [the doors of the sky], because of the heat of the fire beneath where the gods scoop water.

The glide path of Horus,
the glide path of Horus,
will King Unas glide on,
in this heat of the fire where the gods scoop water.

They will make a road for King Unas
(so) that King Unas may pass on it,
for this King Unas is Horus.'

225 (314)
spell against the guardian of the door

by the priest

To say the words :

'Back, gored longhorn,
with the fingers of the horizon on his horns !

Fall down !
Retreat !'

226 (315)
entering the sky

by the King

'Here am I, King Unas, O screeching baboon, O howling baboon. My death is at my own desire, my honour upon me, I make acclamation and ululation and sit among [the youngsters].'

227 (316)

by the King

'O You back-turning star, I, King Unas does not have to give You his magic. I sit side by side with my back to the swept area in Heliopolis. I will be taken to the sky.'

228 (317)

by the King

To say the words :

'I, King Unas, have come here in advance of the waters of the Great Flood. I am Sobek, green of plumage, watchful of face, raised fore, the raging one who came forth from the tigh and tail of the Great One in the Sunshine.

I have come to my canals which in the flood-shore of the Great Inundation, to the place of rest with green fields in the horizon, that I might make green the herbage which is on the shores of the horizon, that I may bring faience to the Great Eye in the midst of the fields. I take my seat which is in the horizon. I appear as Sobek, son of Neith. I will eat with my mouth. I will urinate and I will copulate with my phallus. I am the Lord of Semen, who takes women from their husbands to the place I wish, according to the urges of my heart.'

The Phallus of Babi sails the King
East Wall

229 (318)

by the priest

[*To say the words :*

'King Unas is a Plait-snake, the bull who leads], who swallowed his seven uraei and his seven neck-vertebrae came into being, [who gives orders] to the seven Enneads which hear the word of the monarch.

King Unas will come so that he may inhale myrrh and become beautiful with myrrh, (for) King Unas fingernail is full of myrrh.

King Unas will take away your power, You gods !
Serve King Unas who will assign your Kas.'

230 (319)

by the priest

To say the words :

'King Unas is a Bull with radiance in the midst of his eyes. The mouth of King Unas is hale with the fiery blast and the head of King Unas has the horns of Horus, the Lord of the Nile Valley.

King Unas will lead the god.
King Unas will control the Ennead.
King Unas will cultivate lapis-lazuli.
King Unas will plant the acacia of the Nile Valley, for King Unas has tied the cords of the peppergrass, King Unas

has united the skies, and King Unas has power over the southern and northern lands - the god of those in (his) presence, for King Unas has built the city of the god in accordance with its proper due.

King Unas is the third in his appearance
(with Horus and Re).'

231 (320)

by the priest

To say the words :

'Now that King Unas has cleared the night, and King Unas has sent off the hour-stars, the controlling powers will appear and privilege King Unas as Babi.

King Unas is the son of her who does not know him : she bore King Unas to yellow-face, Lord of the Night Skies.

(He is) your greater, You Lords !
Hide yourselves, You common folk,
from before King Unas !
King Unas is Babi,
Lord of the Night Sky,
the Bull of Baboons,
who lives on those
who do not know him.'

232 (321)

by the priest

To say the words :

'O You (ferryman)
with the back of his head behind him,

bring to King Unas Seferet-hetepet
which is on the back of Osiris,
(so) that King Unas may ascend on it to the sky and
King Unas may escort Re in the sky.'

The lifetime of King Unas is eternal repetition.
His limit is everlastingness.

First Intermediary Period

The Instruction to Merikare

King Khety to his son – beginning is fragmentary – IXth Dynasty – First Intermediary Period – ca.2134 – ? BCE [5]

The prologue and the section on rebellion are fragmentary and have been omitted from the main body of the text, except for the latter's concluding stanzas.

Prologue

[The beginning of the Teaching made by the King of Upper and Lower Egypt, Khety] for his son Merikare.

On Rebellion

(------)

'May You be justified before the god,
that a man may say [even in] your [absence] that You punish in accordance [with the offence] !

(A) good character is a man's heaven, (but) the cursing of the [furious] of heart is painful.

If You are skilled in speech, You will win.
The tongue is (---) and the sword of [the King].

Speaking is stronger than any weapon.
No one can overcome the skillfull heart.

[Teach] your [people] on the mat,
the wise is a [school] to the officials.

Those who know that he knows will not attack him, no [misfortune] occurs when he is near. Justice (or truth) comes to him distilled, like the intentions of the sayings of the ancestors.

Dealing with officals and commoners

Copy your fathers, your ancestors,
work is done [successfully]
with [their] knowledge.
Look, their words endure in writings !
Open, read and copy their knowledge !
He who is taught becomes skilled.
Do not be evil, kindness of heart is good.
Let your memorial last through love of You.
Increase [the corvee-workers], befriend the town-folk,
(and) the god will be praised for the donations, (one will) watch over your (reputation),
praise your goodness,
(and) pray for your health (---).

Respect the officials, sustain your people,
strengthen your borders, your frontier patrols.

It is good to work for the future !
One respects the life of the foresighted,
while the trustful heart fails.

Make people come [to You] through your good nature.
A wretch is who desires the land [of his neighbors].

A fool is who covets what others possess.
Life on Earth passes, it is not long.
Happy is he who is remembered.

A million men do not benefit
the Lord of the Two Lands.
Is there [a man] who lives forever ?
He who comes with Osiris passes (by),
just as he leaves who indulged himself.

Make your officials great,
so that they act by your laws.
He who has wealth at home will not be partial,
(for) he is a rich man who lacks nothing.
The poor man does not speak justly.

One who says : "I wish I had." is unrighteous,
(for) he inclines to him who will pay him.
Great is the man whose great men are great.
Strong is the King who has councillors.
Wealthy is he who is rich in his officials.
Speak truth in your house,
that the officials of the land may respect You.

Righteousness of heart is proper
for the Lord (of the Two Lands).
The front of the house puts awe in the back.

Do justice, then You endure on Earth.
Calm the weeper, do not oppress the widow,
do not expel a man from his father's property,
do not reduce the officials in their possessions.
Beware of punishing wrongfully.

Do not kill, it does not serve You.
Punish with beatings, with detention,
thus will the land be well-ordered.

Except for the rebel,
whose plans are found out,
for the god knows the malcontent of heart.
The god smites the rebels in blood.
He who is merciful [will increase his] lifetime.

Do not kill a man whose excellence You know,
with whom You used to chant the writings,
who was brought up [and recognized] before the god,
with free striding feet in the place of secrets !

The Ba comes to the place it knows,
it does not miss its former path,
no kind of magic holds it back,
it comes to those who give it water.

The court that judges the needy,
You know they are not lenient,
on the day of judging the miserable,
in the hour of doing their task !
It is painful when the accuser has knowledge ...

Let your heart not trust in length of years,
(for) they (re)view a lifetime in an hour !

When, after death, a man remains over,
his deeds are set beside him in a heap,
and being there lasts forever !

A fool is who does what they reprove !
He who reaches them without having done wrong,
will exist there like (a) god, free-striding
like the Lords of Eternity !

Advice on raising troops and religious duties

Raise your young soldiers and the residence will love You. Increase your supporters among the helpers. See, your town is full of new growth.

These twenty years,
the youth has been happy, following its heart.
The [helpers] are now going forth (once again),
[veterans] return to their children (---).
[Indeed they are the old men,]
I raised troops from on my accession.

Make your great ones great,
and promote your [soldiers].
Increase the youth of your following,
equip with amounts, endow with fields,
reward them with herds.
Do not prefer the wellborn to the commoner,
(but) choose a man on account of his skills,
then every work of craft will be done !
Guard your borders, secure your forts,
troops are useful to their Lord.

Make [many] monuments for the god,
this keeps alive their maker's name.

A man should do what profits his Ba : perform the monthly service, wear the white sandals, visit the temple, [be discreet] concerning the secrets, enter the shrine, eat bread in the house of the god, proffer libations, multiply the loaves, make ample the daily offerings. It is good for him who does it.

Endow your monuments
according to your wealth.
Even one day gives to eternity,
(and) an hour contributes to the future.
The god knows the man who works for him,
(even) when your statues are brought to far foreign countries, who do not give them their listed offerings.

The historical section

Diseased and deprived is he who imprisons the evil gang (of rebels), (for) the enemy cannot be calm within Egypt. Troops will fight troops, as the ancestors foretold.

Egypt fought in the necropolis, destroying tombs in vengeful destruction. I did the like, and the like happened, as is done to one who strays from the path of the god ...

Do not deal evilly with the Southland, You know what the residence foretold about it. [As this happened so that may happen.] (But) they have not transgressed like they said ! I attacked Thinis and Maki, opposite its southern border at Tawet.

I engulfed it like a flood ! King Mer(ib)re, the justified, had not done this, (so) be merciful on account of this [to the encumbered].

[Make peace], renew the treaties.
No river lets itself be hidden.
It is good to work for the future.

You stand well with the Southland, they come to You bearing tribute, with gifts. I have acted like the forefathers : if one has no grain to give, be kind, since they are humble before You. Be sated with your bread, your beer ... Granite comes to You unhindered.

Do not despoil the monuments of another, but quarry stone in Tura. Do not build your tomb out of ruins, (using) what had been made for what is to be made.

Behold, the King is the Lord of Joy ! May You rest, sleep in your strength, follow your heart, through what I have done : there is no foe within your borders.

I arose as Lord of the City, whose heart was sad because of the Northland. From Hetshenu to [Sembaqa, and its southern border at Two-Fish Channel.] I pacified the entire West as far as the coast of the Lake. It pays taxes, it gives cedar wood. One sees juniper wood which they give us. The East abounds in bowmen, and their labour-dues [arrive]. The middle islands are turned back, and every man from amongst them. The temples say : "You are greater than I !"

Look, the land they had ravaged has been made into nomes, (and) all kinds of large towns [are in it]. What was ruled by one is in the hands of ten, officials are appointed, (and) tax-[lists drawn up]. When free men are given land, they work for You like a single team. No rebellious heart will arise among them, and Hapy will not fail to come.

The dues of the Northlands are in your hand, for the mooring-post is staked in the destrict I made in the East, from Hebenu to The Ways of Horus. It is settled with towns, filled with people, of the best in the whole land, to repel attacks against them.

May I see a brave man who will do the like, who will add to what I have done. (For) a vile heir would [disgrace] me. But this should be said to the bowmen : "The miserable Asiatic, is wretched because of the place he is in : short of water, bare of wood, its paths are many and painful because of mountains. He does not dwell in one place, (and) food propels his legs. He fights since the time of Horus, not conquering nor being conquered, he does not announce the day of combat, like a thief who hides for a (united) group."

But as I live and shall be what I am, these bowmen were a sealed wall. I breached [their strongholds], I made Lower Egypt attack them, I captured their inhabitants, I seized their cattle, until the Asiatics abhorred Egypt. Do not concern yourself with him, (for) the Asiatic is a crocodile on its shore : it snatches from a lonely road, (but) it cannot seize from a populous town !

Medenyt has been restored to its nome, its one side is irrigated as far as Kem-Wer. It is the [defense] against the bowmen. Its walls are warlike, its soldiers many, its serfs know how to bear arms, apart from the free men within.

The region of Memphis totals ten thousand men, free citizens who are not taxed. Officials are in it since the time it was residence, the borders are firm, the garrisons valiant. Many northerners irrigate it as far as the Northland, taxed with grain in the manner of free men. For those who do this, this is the way to surpass me. Look, it is the gateway of the Northland ! It has acted as a dyke as far as Heracleopolis ! Abundant citizens are the support of the heart. Beware of being surrounded by the serfs of the foe. Caution prolongs life.

If your southern border is attacked, (it means) the bowmen have put on the war belt ! Build buildings in the Northland ! As the name of a man is not made small by his actions, so a settled town is not harmed. Build [a temple for your statue.] The foe loves grieving the heart and vile deeds.

The glory of kingship

King Khety, the justified, laid down in teaching : "He who is silent of heart towards violence diminishes the offerings. The god will attack the rebel for the sake of the temples." He will be overcome for what he has done, he will be sated with what he planned to gain, one will not bring him on one's water on the day of woe.

Enrich the offering tables !
Revere the god !

Do not say : "It is weakness of heart !", and do not - slacken your actions. He who opposes You disturbs the sky. The monuments are sound for a hundred years. If the foe understood this, he would not attack them. (But) there is no one who has no enemy.

The Lord of the Two Shores is one who knows, (and) the King, the Lord of Courtiers, is not foolish, (for) as one (who is) wise did he come from the womb ! From a million men, the god singled him out ...

A goodly office is kingship, it has no son, no brother to maintain its memorial. But one man provides for the other : a man acts for him who was before him, so that what he has done is preserved by his successor.

Look, a shameful deed occured in my time : the nome of Thinis was ravaged ! Though it happened through my doing, I learned it after it was done.

There was retribution for what I had done. For it is evil to destroy, useless to restore what one has damaged, (or) to rebuild what one has demolished. Beware of it ! With its like, a blow is repaid, (and) to every action there is a response.

divine justice

Generation succeeds generation, (while) the god, who knows (their) characters, has hidden himself.

One cannot resist the Lord of the Hand, (for) he reaches all that the eyes can see ...

One should revere the god on his path, made of costly stones, fashioned of bronze.

As watercourse is replaced by watercourse, so no river allows itself to be concealed, (and) it breaks the channel in which it was hidden. So also, the Ba goes to the place it knows, and strays not from its former path.

Make worthy your house of the West, make firm your station in the necropolis, by being upright, by doing justice, upon which the hearts of men rely.

The loaf of the upright is preferred to the ox of the evildoer. Work for the god, he will also work for You : with offerings that make the altar flourish, with cravings that proclaim your name.

The god thinks of him
who works for him !

Hymn to the creator-god

Well tended is humanity,
the cattle of the god :
he made sky and earth for their sake,
he subdued the water monster,
he made breath for their noses to live.
They are his images,
who came from his body.

He shines in the sky for their sake.
He made for them plants and cattle,
fowl and fish to feed them.

He slew his foes, reduced his children,
when they thought of making rebellion.

He makes daylight for their sake,
he sails by to see them.

He has built his shrine around them,
when they weep he hears.
He made for them rulers in the egg,
leaders to raise the back of the weak.

He made for them magic as weapons,
to ward off the blow of events,
watching over them by day and by night.

He has slain the traitors among them,
as a man beats his son
for the sake of his brother.
For the god knows every name.

Epilogue

Do no ill (against) my speech, which lays down all the laws of kingship, which instructs You, that You may rule the land ! And may You reach me with none to accuse You !

Do not kill one who is close to You, whom You have favored, the god knows him. He is one of the fortunate ones on Earth ... (for) divine are they who follow the King !

Make yourself loved by everyone, (for) a good character is remembered.

[When time] has passed, may You be called : "He who ended the time of trouble" by those who come after the House of Khety, [in thinking] of what has come today.

Look, I have told You the best of my thoughts !
Act by what is set before You !'

Middle Kingdom

To Become Magic

Coffin Texts, spell 262 – Middle Kingdom (ca. 1938 – 1759 BCE) [6]

TO BECOME HEKA

O You nobles who are in the presence of the Lord of All. Behold, I have come to You !

Fear me in proportion to what You know !

It is I whom the Sole Lord made before there came into being the two meals on Earth. When he sent forth his Sole Eye. When he was alone. Being what came forth from his own mouth, when his million Kas were the protection of his companions. When he spoke with Khepri, with him, that he might be more powerful than he, and he took Hu upon his mouth.

It is I who am the very son of Her
who gave birth to the All,
born before he had a mother.
I am the protection of what the Sole Lord commanded.
I am he who caused the Ennead to live.
I am he who act as he pleases, the father of the gods, lofty of standard, who makes the gods effective in accordance with the command of Her who gave birth to the All ; the august god who eats and speaks with his mouth.
I have kept silence. I have bowed down.
I have come shod, O Bulls of the Sky.
I have seated myself, O Bulls of Nut, in this my dignity of "Greatest of the owners of Kas", heir of Atum.
I have come that I might take my seat and that I might recieve my dignity, for to me belonged the All before You came into being, You gods.

Go down upon your haunches !
For I am HEKA !

Coffin Texts - spell 261.

Discourse of a Man with his Ba

probably Middle Kingdom XIIth Dynasty (ca.1938 – 1759 BCE) [7]

FIRST section

<first section missing>
<opening lines are torn and incomplete> -------

[My Ba (soul) opened its mouth to me, to answer what I said :]

------ (1) your --- to say ----- [their tongue] will not be partial ----- payment. Their tongue is not partial.

SECOND section

I opened my mouth to my Ba,
to answer what it had said :
This is too much for me today,
that my Ba does not converse with me !
It is too great for exaggeration,
it is like deserting me !
Don't go my Ba !
Attend to me in this ! ------
--- in my body like a net of cord,
but it will not be able to escape
the day of pain !
Behold ! My Ba neglects me.
I do not listen to it !
Drags me toward death before [I] come to it,
casts [me] on fire so as to burn me !

It shall stay close to me on the day of pain !
It shall stand on that side,
like a praise-singer does.
Such is he who goes forth.
He has brought himself.

O my Ba, foolish to belittle the sorrow due to life,
leads me toward death before I come to it !
Sweeten the West for me !
Is that difficult ?

Life is a passage and trees fall.
Trample on wrong, put down my misery !

May Thoth judge me,
he who pacifies the gods !
May Khons defend me,
the scribe of truth !
May Re hear my speech,
even he who conducts the Bark of the Sun !
May Isdes (netherworld judge)
defend me in the Holy Hall !

For my suffering is pressing,
a [weight] too heavy a burden to be borne by me.
It would be a sweet relief,
if the gods drove off my body's secrets !

THIRD section

What my Ba said to me :

'Are You not a man ?
Are You not alive ?

So what do You gain
by complaining about life
like a Lord of Wealth ?'

FOURTH section

I said :

'I have not passed away yet,
but that is not the point !

Surely, if You run away, You will not be cared for, with every criminal saying : "I will seize You." Though You are death, your name lives. Yonder is the place of rest, the heart's goal.

For the West is a dwelling-place, a voyage. If my Ba listens to me without making difficulties, with its heart in accord with me, it shall be happy ! I shall make it reach the West like one who is in his tomb and whose burial a survivor tends.

I shall make a cool shelter over your corpse, so as to make another Ba in oblivion envious ! I shall make a cool shelter, so that You shall not be cold, and will make another Ba who is scorched envious ! I shall quench my thirst at the place at the river over which I made shade, so as to make another Ba who is hungry envious !

But if You lead me toward death in this way, You will not find a place to rest in the West. So be clement, my Ba, my brother, until my heir comes, one who will present the offerings and wait at the tomb on the day of burial, having prepared the bier of the necropolis.'

FIFTH section

My Ba opened its mouth to me,
to answer what I said :

'If You think of burial, it is heartbreak ; it is the gift of tears, causing a man's misery ; it is taking a man from his house, to cast him on the high ground. Then, You will not go up to see the Sunlight.

They who built in granite, who erected halls in excellent tombs of fine construction, so that the builders should become gods, their offering-stones are desolate, like the oblivious dead, who died on the riverbank for lack of a survivor, when the flood has taken its toll, and the Sunlight likewise, to whom only the fishes at the water's edge talk.

Listen to me !
Look, it is good for people to listen.
Follow the happy day and forget worry !

A common man ploughs his plot. He loads his harvest into a boat. He tows the freight, for his feast day is approaching and he saw the darkness of a North wind arise.

He is vigilant in the boat when the Sun sets and gets out with his wife and children, and they perish by a pool infested by night with crocodiles.

When at last he sat down, he broke out, saying : "I do not weep for that mother, for whom there is no coming from the West to be on Earth another time. I grieve for her children broken in the egg, who have seen the face of Khenty before they have lived !"

A common man asks for an early meal. His wife says to him : "It is for supper." He goes outside to relieve himself for a moment. When he turns back to his house, he is like another man, and though his wife pleads with him, he does not hear her, after he has relieved himself, and the household is distraught.'

SIXTH section

I opened my mouth to my Ba,
to answer what it had said :

FIRST CANTO
denial of one's name

'Lo ! My name is loathsome.
Lo ! More than carrion smell
on a summer's day when the sky burns.
Lo ! My name is loathsome.
Lo ! More than a catch of fish
on fishing days when the sky burns.
Lo ! My name is loathsome.
Lo ! More than ducks smell.
More than a clump of reeds full of waterfowl.
Lo ! My name is loathsome.
Lo ! More than fishermen smell.
More than the marsh-pools where they fish.
Lo ! My name is loathsome.
Lo ! More than crocodiles smell.
More than a shore-site full of crocodiles.
Lo ! My name is loathsome.
Lo ! More than that of a wife
about whom lies are told to the husband.
Lo ! My name is loathsome.
Lo ! More than that of a strong youth
who is said to belong to one who rejects him.
Lo ! My name is loathsome.
Lo ! More than the town of a king
that utters sedition behind his back.

SECOND CANTO
denial of the others

To whom shall I speak today ? Brothers are bad,
the friends of today do not love.
To whom shall I speak today ?
Hearts are greedy,
everyone robs his neighbour's goods.
[To whom shall I speak today ?]
Kindness has perished,
violence rules all.

To whom shall I speak today ?
One is content with evil,
goodness is debased everywhere.

To whom shall I speak today ?
He who should enrage decent men
by his crimes is acclaimed by everyone
for his evil deeds.

To whom shall I speak today ?
Men plunder.
Everyone robs his neighbour's goods.

To whom shall I speak today ?
The criminal is an intimate friend.
The brother with whom one dealt is a foe.

To whom shall I speak today ?
Forgotten is the past.
Today one does not help him who helped.

To whom shall I speak today ?
Brothers are evil. One goes to strangers for affection.

To whom shall I speak today ?
Faces are blank.
Everyone turns his face from his brothers.

To whom shall I speak today ?
Hearts are greedy,
there is no heart to put one's trust in.

To whom shall I speak today ?
Gone are the just.
The land is left over to the evildoers.

To whom shall I speak today ?
One lacks an intimate.
One resorts to darkness to complain.

To whom shall I speak today ?
The cheerful heart is gone
and he with whom one walked is no more.

To whom shall I speak today ?
I am burdened with grief
from lack of one who enters the heart.

To whom shall I speak today ?

Wrong roams the Earth,
and there is no end to it.

THIRD CANTO
denial of life and glorification of death

Death is in front of my face today,
[like] health to the sick,
like deliverance from detention.

Death is in front of my face today,
like the flagrance of myrrh,
like a shelter on a windy day.

Death is in front of my face today,
like the flagrance of lotus,
like sitting on the shore of drunkenness.

Death is in front of my face today,
like a well-trodden way,
like coming home from war.

Death is in front of my face today,
like the clearing of the sky,
as when a man grasps what he did not know before.

Death is in front of my face today,
like a man's longing to see his home,
having spent many years in captivity.

FOURTH CANTO

In truth, he who is yonder will be a living god,
punishing the crime of him who does it.

In truth, he who is yonder will stand in the Bark the
Sun, making its bounty flow to the temples.

In truth, he who is yonder will be a wise man, who
cannot, when he speaks, be stopped from appealing to
Re.'

SEVENTH section

What my Ba said to me :

'Throw complaint over the fence,
You my comrade, my brother !
May You make offering upon the brazier,
and cling to life by the means You describe !
Yet love me here, having put aside the West !

But when it is wished that You attain the West, that your body joins the Earth, then I shall alight after You have become weary, and then we shall dwell together.'

Colophon :

It is finished from beginning to end,
as it was found in writing.

The Instruction of Amenemhat

to his son Senusret I – nearly complete – XIIth Dynasty – Middle Kingdom – ca.1909 BCE [8]

PROLOGUE

Beginning of the instruction made by the Majesty of King Sehetepibre, son of Re, Amenemhat, the justified, as he spoke in a mission of truth, to his son the All-Lord.

THE TEACHING

address to Senusret

He said : 'Risen as god, hear what I tell You, (so) that You may rule the land, govern the shores, (and) increase well-being !

beware of nobodies

Beware of subjects who are nobodies,
of whose plotting one is not aware.

Do not go near to them alone.
Trust not a brother, know not a friend,
make no intimates, it is worthless.

When You lie down, guard your heart yourself.
For no man has adherents on the day of woe.

by doing good one does not avoid an attack

I gave to the beggar, I raised the orphan,
I gave to those who were nothing,
like to those who were something.

But he who ate my food raised opposition, he whom I gave my hands, used them to assail me, wearers of my fine linen looked at me as if they were needy, those perfumed with my myrrh [poured water while wearing it.]

remember what has happened

You my living peers, my partners among men, make for me mourning such as has not been heard, for so great a combat had not yet been seen ! If one fights in the arena forgetful of the past, success will elude him who ignores what he should know.

the narrative of the assassination

It was after supper, night had come. I was taking an hour of rest, lying on my bed, for I was weary. As my heart began to follow sleep, weapons for my protection were turned against me, while I was like a snake of the desert. I awoke at the fighting, [came to myself], and found it was a combat of the guard. Had I quickly seized weapons in my hand, I would have made the cowards retreat. But no one is strong at night ; no one can fight alone ; no success is achieved without a helper.

Thus bloodshed occurred while I was without You ; before the courtiers had heard I would hand over to You ; before I had sat with You so as to advise You. For I had not prepared for it, had not expected it, had not foreseen the failing of the servants ... the exceptional nature of this murder.

Had women (of the harem) ever marshaled troops ? Are rebels nurtured inside the palace ? [Or did destroyers break into the place ?] [(It is) a bad memory because of what these miserable people did.] No harm had come to me since my birth, (and) no one equaled me as a doer of deeds.

the confession of excellence

I journeyed to Yebu, I returned to the Delta. Having stood on the land's borders, I observed its interior. I reached the borders of the strongholds ; by my strength and my being.

I was grain-maker, beloved of Nepri.
Hapy honored me on every field.

None hungered in my years.
None thirsted in them.

One sat because I acted and spoke of myself :
I had assigned everything to its place.

I subdued lions, I captured crocodiles,
I repressed those of Wawat,
I captured the Medjay,
I made the Asiatics do the dog walk.

preparing his son

I built myself a house decked with gold, its ceiling of lapis lazuli, walls of silver, floors of [acacia wood], doors of copper, bolts of bronze. The serfs (however) plotted against me.

Be prepared against this !
If You know this,
then You are its Lord,
You the All-Lord.

Behold, much hatred is in the streets. The wise says "yes", the fool says "no" (for) he has not understood it, (as) his face is lacking (eyes), (that You) were my own tongue, Senusret my son, when I (still) walked on my feet, (that You) were my own heart, when my eyes (still) beheld You, the child of a happy hour.

concluding advise ?

Behold, I made the beginning, You will tie the end. I have landed by the dead, (and) You wear the White Crown of a god's son. The seal is in its correct place, (and) jubilation has started for You in the bark of Re.

Ascend to the throne
for a government better than most,
not like mine !

Be courageous,
raise your monuments,
establish your strongholds,
and beware of those You know,
for I do not wish them
on the side of your Majesty.'

Wedjat or Eye of Horus

New Kingdom

The Great Hymn to the Aten

by Akhenaten – ca. 1353 – 1336 BCE – in the Tomb of Ay – West Wall [9]

Adoration of
Re-Harakhti-who-rejoices-in-lightland
In-his-name-Shu-who-is-Aten, living forever ;
the great living Aten, who is in jubilee,
Lord of all that the Disk surrounds,
Lord of the Sky,
Lord of the Earth,
Lord of the House-of-Aten
in Akhet-Aten.

Adoration of the King
of Upper and Lower Egypt,
who lives by Ma'at,
the Lord of the Two Lands,
Nefer-kheperu-Re,
Sole-one-of-Re,
the Son of Re who lives by Ma'at,
Lord of Crowns,
Akhenaten, great in his lifetime
and of the beloved great Queen,

Lady of the Two Lands :
Nefer-nefru-Aten Nefertiti,
who lives in health and youth forever !

The Vizier, the Fanbearer
on the right of the King ---

he says :

The Hymn

THE ATEN AS RE WITH HIS COURSE

morning beauty

'Splendid You rise in the lightland of the sky,
O living Aten, creator of life !
You have dawned in the eastern lightland.
You fill every land with your beauty.

noon dominion

You are beauteous, mighty and radiant.
Risen high over every land.
Your rays embrace the lands,
to the limit of all that You made.
Being Re, You reach their end.
You bend them for your beloved son.
Though You are far, your rays are on Earth.

Though seen by them,
your course is unknown.

night chaos

When You set in the western lightland,
Earth is in darkness, as if death.
The sleepers are in their chambers, heads covered,
no eye seeing the other.
One could steal their goods from under their heads,
they would not notice it.
Every lion comes from its den.
The serpents bite.
Darkness hovers, Earth is silent.

For its creator rests in the lightland.

dawn rebirth

At dawn You have risen in the lightland.
So shine as the Aten of daytime !
You dispel the dark and cast your rays.
The Two Lands celebrate daily.
Awake they stand on their feet.
You have made them get up.
They wash and dress, their arms raised
in adoration to your appearance.
The entire land sets out to work.
All cattle are satisfied with their fodder.
The trees and the grass become green.
Birds fly from their nests,
their wings praising your Ka.
All game animals frisk on their hooves,
all that fly and flutter,
live when You dawn for them.
Ships fare downstream and back upstream,
roads lie open when You rise.
The fish in the river dart before You.
Your rays penetrate the Great Green Deep.

WORKS AND NATURE OF THE ATEN

the child

O You, who make semen grow in women,
who creates people from sperm,
who feeds the son in his mother's womb,
who soothes him to still his tears.

You nurse in the womb !

Giver of breath to nourish all creatures.
When the child emerges from the womb
to breathe on the day of his birth,
You open wide his mouth to supply his needs.

the chicken

The chick in the egg, chirping in the shell,
You give it breath within to sustain its life.
When it is complete,
it breaks out from the egg.
It emerges from the egg, to say it is complete.
Walking on its legs when emerging.

the Aten as doer
un-saying, solitary, omnipotent

How many are your deeds,
though hidden from sight.

O Sole God without equal !

You made the Earth as You desired, You alone.
With people, cattle, and all creatures.
With everything upon Earth that walks on legs,
and all that is on high and flies with its wings.

the Two Niles :

The foreign lands of Syria and Nubia, and the land of Egypt, You set everybody in his place and supply their needs. They all have their food and their lifetimes are counted. Tongues differ in speech, their characters as well.

Their skins are distinct,
for You distinguished the peoples.
You made the Nile in the Netherworld.
You bring it up when You will,
to keep those of Egypt alive,
for You have created them for yourself.
Lord of All who toils for them.
Lord of All Lands who shines for them.
O Aten of daytime, great in glory !

All distant lands, You make them live.
You made a heavenly Nile descend for them.
With waves beating on the mountains
like the sea,
to drench their fields and their towns.

How excellent are your ways,
O Lord of Eternity !
The Nile from heaven for foreign peoples
and all land-creatures that walk on legs.
For Egypt the Nile from the Netherworld.

THEOLOGY OF THE ATEN

life-giving nature of Aten

Your rays nurse all fields.
When You shine they live, they grow for You.
You made the seasons,
so that all that You made may come to life.
Winter cools them,
and heat makes them sense You.

the Aten is sole witness, creator and presence

You created the sky
far away in order to ascend to it,
to witness everything You created.

You are alone, shining
in your form of the living Aten.
Risen, radiant, distant and near.

You made millions of forms
from yourself alone :
cities, towns, fields, the river's course.
All eyes see You above them
as the Aten of the daytime on high.
When You are gone, (...) your eye is gone (...)
which You have made (?) [for their sake]

Pharaoh as exclusive mediator

But even then You are in my heart
and there is no other who knows You,
only your son, Nefer-kheperu-Re,
Sole-one-of-Re,
whom You have taught
your ways and your might.

The ones on Earth
come into being by your hand,
in the way You made them.
When You rise, they live.
When You set, they die.
You yourself are lifetime itself,
one lives through You.
All eyes rest on beauty until You set.
All labor ceases when You rest in the West.
When You rise,
You make all arms firm for the King,
every leg is on the move
since You founded the Earth,
You rouse them for your son,
who emerged from your body.
The King who lives by Ma'at,
the Lord of the Two Lands :
Nefer-kheperu-Re, Sole-one-of-Re,

the Son of Re who lives by Ma'at,
the Lord of Crowns,
Akhenaten, great in his lifetime.

And the great Queen whom he loves,
the Lady of the Two Lands :

Nefer-neferu-Aten Nefertiti,
who lives and is rejuvenated
forever and ever.'

hands of Akhenaten and Nefertiti
Berlin Museum

Hymns to Amun

Papyrus Leiden I 350 – chapters 80, 90, 100, 200 & 300 –
anonymous priests of Amun at Thebes – ca. 1213 BCE [10]

Chapter 80

The Eight were your first manifestation,
until You completed these, You being Single.

Secret was your body among the elders,
and You kept yourself hidden as Amun,
at the head of the gods.

You made your manifestations in ta-Tenen,
to accompany the primeval ones
in your first primeval time.

Your beauty arose as the Bull of His Mother.
You withdrew as the one in the sky,
enduring as Re.

You returned in fathers, maker of their sons,
to make an excellent heritage for your children.

You began manifestation with nothing,
without the world being empty of You
on the first occasion.

All gods came into existence after You ...

[remainder lost]

Chapitre 80

L'Ogdoade fut Ta première forme,
jusqu'à ce que Tu eusses accompli cela,
demeurant seul.

Mystérieux était Ton corps parmi les ancients.
Comme Amon, qui est à la tête des dieux,
Tu T'étais caché Toi-même.

Tu a créé Tes formes en ta-Tenen
pour accompagner les primordiaux
dans Ton temps primordial.

Ta beauté fut dressée
en tant que Taureau de Sa Mère.
Tu T'es éloigné en habitant au ciel,
Toi qui demeures Re.

Tu ne cesses de venir dans les pères
qui créént leurs enfants,
créant un héritage bienfaisant pour Tes enfants.

Tu commenças à venir à l'existence
alors qu'il n'y avait pas d'être,
mais que le pays n'était pas vide de Toi,
la première fois,
car tous les dieux vinrent
à l'existence après Toi,
[suite perdue]

Chapter 90

The Ennead combined is your body.
Every god joined in your body, is your image.
You emerged first, You inaugurated from the start.
Amun, whose name is hidden from the gods.
Oldest elder, more distinguished than these,
ta-Tenen, who formed [Himself] by Himself
as Ptah.

The toes of His body are the Eight.
He appeared as Re, from Nun,
so that He might rejuvenate.
He sneezed, [as Atum, from] His
[mouth and gave birth to]
Shu and Tefnut, combined in manifestation.
He appears on His throne as His heart prompts.
Who, through His [power],
rules for Himself all that is.
Who binds together for Himself
the kingship for ever,
down to eternity, established as Sole Lord.

Light was His coming into existence
on the first occasion,
with all that exists in stillness for awe of Him.
He honked by voice, as the Great Honker,
coming into a land that He created for Himself,
while He was Alone.
He began speaking in the midst of silence,
opening every eye and causing them to look.
He began crying out
while the world was in stillness,
His yell circulated while He had no second,
so that He might give birth to what is and cause them
to live, and cause every man to know the way to walk.
Their hearts live when they see Him.
His are the effective forms of the Ennead.

Chapitre 90

L'Ennéade réunie est Ton corps.
Chaque dieu uni à Ton corps est Ton image.
Tu T'es révélé le premier,
Tu as inauguré le commencement,
Amon dont le nom est caché aux dieux.
Vieillard plus ancien qu'eux,
ta-Tenen qui s'est formé Lui-même
en tant que Ptah.
Les orteils de Son corps sont l'Ogdoade.

Il apparaît glorieux comme Re hors du Nun
pour qu'Il renouvelle Sa jeunesse.
Il cracha [comme Atum] de Sa
[bouche, et donna naissance à]
Shou et Tefnout, en manifestations combinées.
Il apparaît sur Son trône
selon que Son coeur L'y porte.
Il régit tout ce qui existe par Sa (puissance).
Il organise pour Lui-même,
une royauté pour toujours
jusqu'à l'éternité,
établi comme unique Seigneur.

Lumière était Sa venue à l'existence
pour la première fois
avec tout être en stupeur devant Son prestige.

Il fit retentir Son cri, Lui le crieur véritable,
en venant sur un terrain
qu'Il avait créé étant seul.
Il articula les paroles au milieu du silence.
Il ouvrit tout oeil et fit en sorte qu'ils voient.
Il commença à crier alors que la terre
était dans le silence.

Son rugissement se répercuta
alors qu'il n'y avait aucun être (avec Lui).
Ce qu'Il avait engendré, Il le fit vivre.
Il fit que chacun connaisse la route où marcher.
Leurs coeurs vivent quand ils Le voient.
A Lui appartiennent
les formes effectives de l'Ennéade.

Chapter 100

The One who initiated existence
on the first occasion,
Amun, who developed in the beginning,
whose origin is unknown.

No god came into being prior to Him.
No other god was with Him
who could say what He looked like.

He had no mother who created His name.
He had no father to beget Him or to say :
'This belongs to me.'

Who formed His own egg.
Power of secret birth,
who created His (own) beauty.

Most Divine God,
who came into being Alone.
Every god came into being
since He began Himself.

Chapitre 100

Celui qui a inauguré
l'existence la premiere fois,
Amon, qui est venu à l'existence
au commencement,
sans que Son surgissement soit connu !

Il n'y eut pas de dieu
qui vint à l'existence avant Lui.
Il n'y avait pas d'autre dieu avec Lui
pour exprimer Ses formes.

Il n'y avait pas de mère
qui Lui ait fait Son nom.

Il n'y avait pas de père
qui L'ait engendré et qui ait dit :
'C'est moi !'
Il est Celui qui a façonné Son oeuf Lui-même,
le Puissant dont la naissance est mystérieuse,
qui a créé Sa beauté.

(Il est) le Dieu Divin
qui est venu à l'existence Lui-même.

Tous les dieux vinrent à l'existence
lorsqu'Il Se donna le commencement.

Chapter 200

Secret of manifestations and sparkling of shape.
Marvellous God, rich in forms.

All gods boast of Him,
to magnify themselves in His beauty,
to the extent of His Divinity.

Re himself is united with His body.
He is the Great One in Heliopolis.

He is called ta-Tenen.
Amun, who comes out of the Nun,
to guide the peoples.

Another of His forms are the Eight,
primeval one of the primeval ones,
begetter of Re.
He completed himself as Atum,
being of one body with him.

He is the Universal Lord,
who initiated that which exists.

His soul, they say, is the one who is in the sky.
He is the one who is in the Netherworld,
foremost of the East.

His Soul is in the sky, His body in the West.
His statue is in southern Heliopolis,
elevating His body.

One is Amun,
who keeps Himself concealed from them,
who hides Himself from the gods,
no one knowing His nature.

He is more remote than the sky,
He is deeper than the Netherworld.

None of the gods knows His true form.
His image is not unfolded in the papyrus rolls.
Nothing certain is testified about Him.

He is too secretive
for His Majesty to be revealed,
He is too great to be enquired after,
too powerful to be known.

People immediately fall
face to face into death
when His Name is uttered
knowingly or unknowingly.

There is no god able to invoke Him by it.
He is soul-like,
hidden of name,
like His secrecy.

Chapitre 200

Mystérieux d'existence,
resplendissant de formes,
Dieu merveilleux aux multiples existences
chaque dieu se glorifie en Lui,
pour se magnifier de Sa perfection
parce qu'Il est Divin.
Rê lui-même s'est uni à Son corps.
Il est le grand dans Héliopolis.
On L'appelle ta-Tenen,
Amon, sorti du Nun, guide des humains.

Une autre de Ses formes est l'Ogdoade
qui engendre les dieux primordiaux
qui donnent naissance à Re.

Il s'accomplit en Atoum
n'étant qu'un seul corps avec lui.
Il est le Seigneur Universel,
le commencement des êtres.

C'est Son Ba, dit-on,
qui est dans le ciel lointain.
Lui-même est dans la Douat
et le Premier de l'Orient.

Son Ba est dans le ciel,
Son corps dans l'Occident.
Sa statue est dans Heliopolis
et élève Son corps.

Unique est Amon
qui Se cache d'eux,
qui Se dérobe aux dieux,
sans que l'on connaisse Son aspect.

Il est plus éloigné que le ciel.
Il est plus profond que la Douat.

Aucun dieu ne connaît Sa véritable nature.
Son image n'est pas étalée dans les écrits.
On n'a point sur Lui de témoignage parfait.

Il est trop mystérieux
pour que soit découverte
Sa prestigieuse majesté.
Il est trop grand pour être interrogé,
trop puissant pour être connu.

On tomberait à l'instant mort d'effroi
si on prononçait Son nom secret,
intentionnellement ou non.

Aucun dieu ne sait L'appeler par ce nom.
Ba caché est Son nom,
tant Il est mystérieux.

Chapter 300

All the gods are three :
Amun, Re and Ptah, without their second.

His identity is hidden as Amun,
He is Re as face, His body is Ptah.

Their towns are on Earth,
fixed for the span of eternity :
Thebes, Heliopolis and Memphis
are established perennially.

When a message is sent from the sky,
it is heard in Heliopolis,
and repeated in Memphis
for the god-with-the-beautiful-face,
put in a report, in Thoth's writing,
directed to the town of Amun, bearing their concerns,
and the matter is answered in Thebes, by an oracle
emerging, intended for the Ennead.

Everything that comes from His mouth,
the gods are bound by it,
according to what has been decreed.

When a message is sent,
it is for killing or for giving life.
Life and death depend on Him for everyone,
except for Him,
Amun,
together with Re, [and Ptah] : total, 3.

Chapitre 300

Trois sont tous les dieux,
Amon, Re, Ptah,
qui n'ont pas de semblable.
Son nom est caché en tant qu'Amon ;
Il est Re par le visage ;
Son corps c'est Ptah.

Leurs villes, dans le pays,
sont établies pour l'éternité :
Thèbes, Héliopolis, Memphis
sont destinées à la pérennité.

Lorsqu'un message est envoyé du ciel
on l'entend à Héliopolis,
on le répète à Memphis
pour le (dieu)-au-beau-visage ;
on l'enregistre dans les écritures de Thoth
pour la ville d'Amon, cela étant de leur compétence.
Les desseins (divins) sont donnés en réponse à Thèbes.

La Parole Divine sort et elle est l'Ennéade.
Tout ce qui sort de la bouche d'Amon,
les dieux sont établis d'après cela, selon Ses ordres.
Le Message Divin,
c'est pour tuer ou pour donner la vie.

Vie et mort dépendent de Lui pour tout homme,
excepté Lui, (Amun)
ensemble avec Re [et Ptah],
au total trois.

Amun, King of the Gods
Louvre

The Shabaka Stone

papyrus copied on stone by Shabaka (ca. 712 – 698 BCE) – original ca. 1292 – 1075 BCE (XIXth – XXth Dynasty) [11]

Shabaka Stone – *British Museum* (498)

SECTION I

The living Horus : excellent Two Lands ;
the Two Ladies : excellent Two Lands ;
the Golden Horus : excellent Two Lands ;
King of Upper and Lower Egypt : Neferkare, the son of Re, [Shabaka], beloved of Ptah-South-of-his-Wall, who lives like Re forever.

This writing was copied out anew by his Majesty in the House of his father Ptah-South-of-his-Wall, for his Majesty found it to be a work of the ancestors which was worm-eaten, so that it could not be understood from beginning to end. His Majesty copied it anew so that it became better than it had been before, in order that his name might endure and his monument last in the House of his father Ptah-South-of-his-Wall throughout eternity, as a work done by the son of Re [Shabaka] for his father Ptah Tenen, so that he might live forever.

SECTION II

He is this Ptah who proclaims by the great name : ta-Tenen. He who united this land of the South as King of Upper Egypt and this land of the Delta as King of Lower Egypt.

He indeed begat Atum who gave birth to the Ennead.

SECTION III

Geb commanded that the Ennead gather to him. He judged between Horus and Seth ; he ended their quarrel. He installed Seth as King of Upper Egypt in the land of Upper Egypt, at the place where he was born, in Su.

And Geb made Horus King of Lower Egypt in the land of Lower Egypt, at the place where his father was drowned which is the 'Division-of-the-Two-Lands' (Memphis).

Thus Horus stood over one region, and Seth stood over one region. They made peace over the Two Lands at Ayan (opposite Cairo). That was the division of the Two Lands.

Geb's words to Seth :
'Go to the place in which You were born.'
Seth : Upper Egypt.
Geb's words to Horus :
'Go to the place in which your father was drowned.'
Horus : Lower Egypt.
Geb's words to Horus and Seth :

'I have separated You.'
--- Lower and Upper Egypt.

Then it seemed wrong to Geb that the portion of Horus was like the portion of Seth.

So Geb gave Horus his inheritance, for he is the son of his firstborn son.

Geb's words to the Ennead :
'I have appointed Horus, the firstborn.'
Geb's words to the Ennead :
'Him alone, Horus, the inheritance.'
Geb's words to the Ennead :
'To his heir, Horus, my inheritance.'
Geb's words to the Ennead :
'To the son of my son, Horus, the Jackal of Upper Egypt ---
Geb's words to the Ennead :
'The firstborn, Horus, the Opener-of-the-ways.'
Geb's words to the Ennead :
'The son who was born --- Horus, on the birthday of the Opener-of-the-ways.'

Then Horus stood over the land. He is the uniter of this land, proclaimed in the great name : ta-Tenen, South-of-his-Wall, Lord of Eternity. Then sprouted the two Great in Magic upon his head. He is Horus who arose as King of Upper and Lower Egypt, who united the Two Lands in the Nome of the (White) Wall, the place in which the Two Lands were united. Reed (heraldic plant for Upper Egypt) and papyrus (heraldic plant for Lower Egypt) were placed on the double door of the House of Ptah. That means : Horus and Seth, pacified and united. They fraternized so as to cease quarreling wherever they may be, being united in the House of Ptah, the 'Balance of the Two Lands' in which Upper and Lower Egypt had been weighed. This is the land ---

--- the burial of Osiris in the House of Sokar.
--- Isis and Nephthys without delay,
for Osiris had drowned in his water.
Isis [and Nephthys] looked out.
Horus speaks to Isis and Nephthys :
'Hurry, grasp him ---.'

Isis and Nephthys speak to Osiris :
'We come, we take You ---.'
--- and brought him to
--- the Earth
at the royal fortress, to the North of ---.
There was built the royal fortress ---.

Geb speaks to Thoth : ------
[Geb] speaks to Isis : ---
Isis causes [Horus and Seth] to come.
Isis speaks to Horus and Seth : '---.'
Isis speaks to Horus and Seth :
"Make peace ---.'
Isis speaks to Horus and Seth :
'Life will be pleasant for You when ---.'
Isis speaks to Horus and Seth :
'It is he who dries your tears ---.'
Isis speaks to ------

The Memphis Theology

SECTION IV

The gods who manifest in Ptah :

Ptah-on-the-Great-Throne, ---
[Ptah] --- who bore the gods.
Ptah-Nun, the father who gave birth to Atum.

[Ptah] --- who bore the gods.
Ptah-Naunet, the mother who bore Atum ;
[Ptah] --- (who bore the gods).
Ptah-the-Great, heart (mind) and tongue (speech) of

the Ennead ;
[Ptah] --- Nefer-Tem at the nose of Re every day.

SECTION V
The LOGOS section

There comes into being in the heart ;
there comes into being by the tongue
(something) as the image of Atum !

Ptah is the very great,
[who gives life to all the gods] and their Kas.
Lo, through this heart and this tongue.

Horus came into being in him (and)
Thoth came into being in him as Ptah.

Power came into being in the heart and by the tongue and in all limbs, according to the teaching that it (the heart) is in all bodies and it (the tongue) is in every mouth of all gods, all men, all flocks, all creeping things and whatever lives ; thinking whatever the heart wishes and commanding whatever the tongue wishes !

His (Ptah's) Ennead is before him as heart, authoritative utterance, teeth, semen, lips and hands of Atum.

This Ennead of Atum came into being through his semen and through his fingers.

Surely, this Ennead (of Ptah) is the teeth and the lips in the mouth, proclaiming the names of all things, from which Shu and Tefnut came forth as him, and which gave birth to the Ennead (of Ptah).

The sight of the eyes, the hearing of the ears, and the breathing of air through the nose, they transmit to the heart, which brings forth every decision. Indeed, the tongue thence repeats what is in front of the heart.

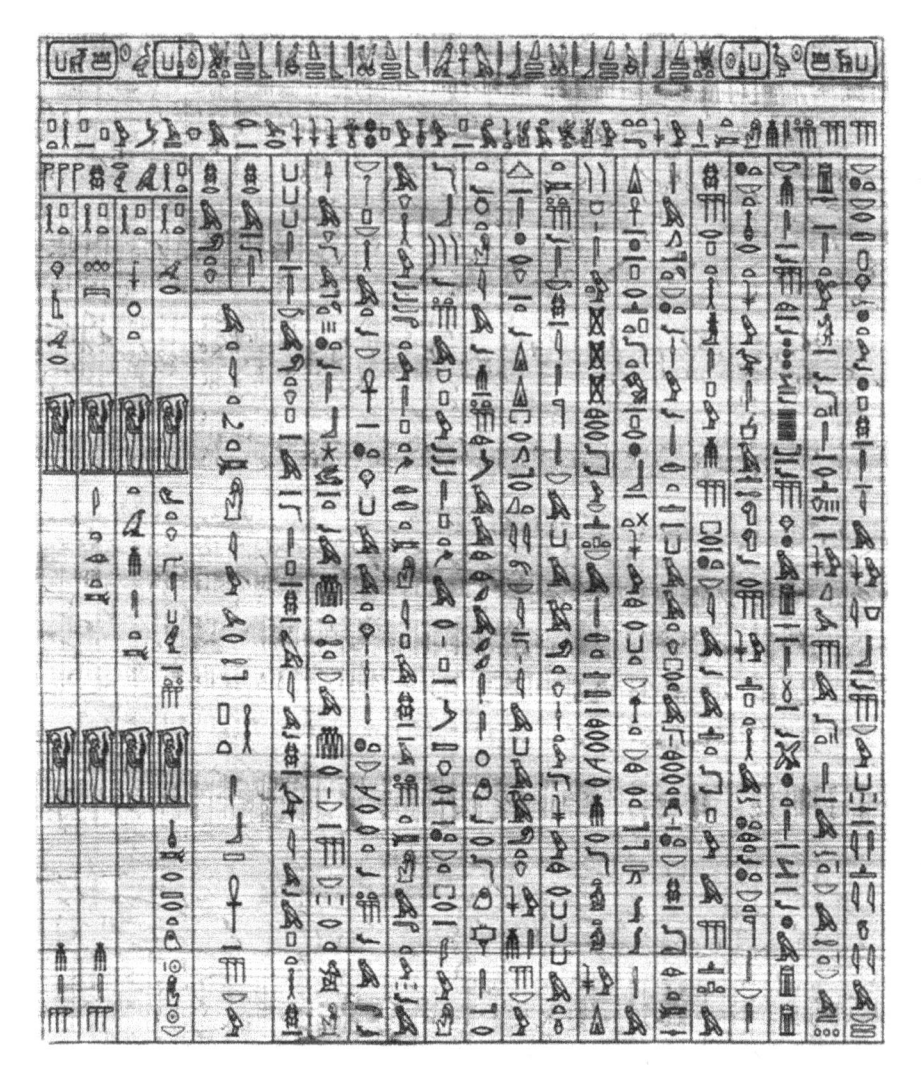

The Memphis Theology

Thus was given birth to all the gods. His (Ptah's) Ennead was completed.

Lo, every word of the god came into being through the thoughts in the heart and the command by the tongue. Thus all witnessing faculties were made and all qualities determined, they that make all foods and all provisions, through this word.

[Justice] to him who does what is loved, [and punishment] to him who does what is hated. Thus life is given to the peaceful and death is given to the criminal.

Thus all labour, all crafts, the action of the arms, the motion of the legs, the movements of all the limbs, according to this command, which is divised by the heart and comes forth by the tongue and creates the performance of everything.

There came the saying that Atum, who created the gods, said concerning Ptah-Tenen : 'He gave birth to the gods.'

From him every thing came forth :
foods, provisions, divine offerings, all good things. Thus Thoth knew and recorded that he is the mightiest of the gods. Thus Ptah was satisfied after he had made all things and all divine words.

Lo, he gave birth to the gods, he made the towns, he established the nomes, he placed the gods in their shrines, he settled their offerings, he established their shrines, he made their bodies according to their wishes. Thus the gods entered into their bodies of every kind of wood, of every kind of stone, of every kind of clay, in every kind of thing that grows upon him in which they came to be.

Thus all the gods and their Kas were gathered to him, content and united with the Lord of the Two Lands.

SECTION V

The Great Throne (Memphis) that gives joy to the heart of the gods in the House of Ptah is the granary of ta-Tenen, the mistress of all life, through which the sustenance of the Two Lands is provided, owing to the fact that Osiris was drowned in his water, Isis and Nephthys looked out, beheld him, and attended to him, Horus quickly commanded Isis and Nephthys to grasp

Osiris and prevent his drowning.

They heeded in time and brought him to land. He entered the secret portals in the glory of the Lords of Eternity, in the steps of him who rises in the horizon, on the ways of Re at the Great Throne.

He entered the palace and joined the gods of ta-Tenen Ptah, Lord of Years. Thus Osiris came into the Earth at the Royal Fortress, to the North of this land to which he had come.

His son Horus arose as King of Upper Egypt, arose as King of Lower Egypt, in the embrace of his father Osiris and of the gods in front of him and behind him.

statue of Ptah
tomb of Tutankhamun

The Instruction of Amen-em-apt

for his son Hor-em-maakher – complete XIX / XXth Dynasty – New Kingdom – ca.1292 – 1075 BCE [12]

PROLOGUE

the book

Beginning of the teaching for life,
the instructions for well-being,
every rule for relations with elders, (and)
for conduct toward magistrates.

Knowing how to answer one who speaks,
to reply to one who sends a message,
so as to direct him on the paths of life,
to make him prosper upon earth,
to let his heart enter its shrine,
steering (it) clear of evil,
to save him from the mouth of strangers,
to let (him) be praised in the mouth of men.

the author

Made by the overseer of fields, experienced in his office, the offspring of a scribe of Egypt. The overseer of grains, who controls the wedjat-measure, who sets the harvest dues for his Lord, who registers the islands of new land, in the great name of his Majesty, who records the markers on the borders of fields, who acts for the King in his listing of taxes, who makes the land-register of the Black Land.

The scribe who determines the offerings for all the gods, who gives land-leases to the people, the overseer of grains, [provider of] foods, who supplies the granary with grains.

The truly silent in Thinite Ta-wer, the justified in Ipu, who owns a pyramid on the west of Senu, who has a chapel at Abydos, Amen-em-apt, the son of Kanakht, the justified in Ta-wer.

the addressee

(For) his son, the youngest of his children,
the smallest of his family,
the devotee of Min-Kamutef,
the water-pourer of Wennofer,
who places Horus on his father's throne,
who [guards] him in his noble shrine, who ---
the watcher of the mother of god,
inspector of the black cattle
of the terrace of Min,
who protects Min in his shrine :
Hor-em-maakher is his true name,
child of a nobleman of Ipu,
son of the sistrum-player of Shu and Tefnut,
and chief musician of Horus, Tawosre.

He says :

THE TEACHING

Chapter 1 : the charge to his son

'Give your ears, hear the sayings,
give your heart to understand them.

It is good to put them in your heart, (but)
woe to him who neglects them !
Let them rest in the casket of your belly,
may they be bolted in your heart.
When there rises a whirlwind of words,
they will be a mooring-post for your tongue.

If You make your life with these in your heart,
You will find it a success.
You will find my words a storehouse for life,
(and) your body will be well upon earth.

Chapter 2 : do not steal

Beware of robbing a poor wretch,
of attacking a cripple.
Do not stretch out your hand to touch an old man,
nor [snatch (at) the word of] a great one.
Do not let yourself be sent on a wicked errand,
nor be friends with him who does it.
Do not raise an outcry against one who attacks
You, nor return him an answer yourself.
He who does evil, the shore rejects him,
its floodwater carries him away,
the north wind comes down to end his hour,
it mingles with the thunderstorm, (and)
the storm cloud is tall,
the crocodiles are vicious.
You heated man, how are You now ?
He cries out, his voice reaches heaven.
It is the Moon who declares his crime.
Steer, (so that) we may ferry the wicked (over),
(as) we do not act like his kind !
Lift him up, give him your hand,
commit him (in) the hands of the god.
Fill his belly with bread of your own,
that he be sated and see.

Another thing good in the heart of the god :
to pause before speaking.

Chapter 3 : prudence in speech

Do not start a quarrel with a hot-mouthed man,
nor needle him with words.
Pause before an intruder, bend before an attacker,
sleep (on it) before speaking.
A storm that bursts like fire in straw,
such is the heated man in his hour.
Withdraw from him, leave him alone.
The god knows how to answer him.
If You make your life with these (words) in your heart,
Your children will observe them.

Chapter 4 : the two types of men

As to the heated man in the temple,
he is like a tree growing [indoors], (only)
a moment lasts its growth of [shoots], (and)
its end comes about in the [woodshed], (or)
it is floated far from its place,
the flame is its burial shroud.
The truly silent, who keeps apart,
he is like a tree grown in a meadow.
it greens, it doubles its yield,
it stands in front of its Lord,
its fruit is sweet, its shade delightful,
its end is reached in the garden.

Chapter 5 : honest and tranquil service

Do not falsify the temple rations.
Do not grasp and You will find profit.
Do not remove a servant of god,
so as to do favours to another.
Do not say : "Today is like tomorrow."
How will this end ?
Comes tomorrow, today has vanished.
The deep has become the water's edge.
Crocodiles are bared, hippopotami stranded.
The fish crowded together.

Jackals are sated, birds are in feast.
The fishnets have been drained.
But all the silent in the temple,
they say : "Re's blessing is great !"
Cling to the silent, then You find life, (and)
your being will prosper upon earth.

Chapter 6 : steal no land and eat from your field

Do not move the markers
on the borders of fields.
Nor shift the position of the measuring-cord.
Do not be greedy for a cubit of land.
Nor encroach on the boundaries of a widow.

The trodden furrow worn down by time,
he who disguises it in the fields,
when he has snared (it) by false oaths,
he will be caught by the might of the Moon.

Recognize him who does this on earth !
He is an oppressor of the weak,
a foe working to destroy your body.
The taking of life is in his eye,
his house is an enemy to the town,
his barns will be destroyed,
his wealth will be seized
from his children's hands, (and)
his possessions will be given to another.

Beware of destroying the borders of fields,
lest a terror carry You away.
One pleases god with the might of the Lord,
when one discerns the borders of fields.

Desire your being to be sound.
Beware of the Lord of All !
Do not erase another's furrow,
it profits You to keep it sound.
Plow your fields

and You will find what You need,
You will receive bread from your own threshing-floor.

Better is a bushel given You by the god,
than five thousand through wrongdoing.
They stay not a day in bin and barn,
they make no food for the beer jar.
A moment is their stay in the granary,
comes morning, (and) they have vanished.
Better is poverty in the hand of the god,
than wealth in the storehouse.
Better is bread with a happy heart,
than wealth with vexation.

Chapter 7 : seek no wealth

Do not set your heart on wealth !
There is no ignoring Shay and Renenet !
Do not let your heart go straying, (for)
every man comes to his hour.
Do not labour to seek increase,
what You have, let it suffice You.
If riches come to You by theft,
they will not stay the night with You.
Comes morning,
(and) they are not in your house ;
their place is seen but they are not there :
earth opened its mouth,
leveled them, swallowed them,
and made them sink into Duat, (or)
they made a hole as big as their size,
and sank into the netherworld, (or)
they made themselves wings like geese,
and flew away to the sky.

Do not rejoice in wealth from theft,
nor complain of being poor.
If the leading archer presses forward,
his company abandons him !
The boat of the greedy is left (in) the mud,

while the bark of the tranquil sails with the wind.
You shall pray to the Aten when he rises,
saying : "Grant me well-being and health !"
He will give You your needs for this life,
and You will be safe from fear.

Chapter 8 : speak no evil

Set your goodness in the belly of men,
then You are greeted by all.
One welcomes the Uraei-serpents.
One spits upon the Apopis-snake.

Guard your tongue from harmful speech,
then You will be loved by others.
You will find your place in the temple.
You will share in the bread-offerings of your Lord.
When You are revered and your coffin conceals You,
You will be safe from the power of god.

Do not shout "crime" against a man,
when the cause of (his) flight is hidden.
Whether You hear something good or evil,
do it outside where it is not heard.
Put the good remark on your tongue,
while the bad is concealed in your belly.

Chapter 9 : avoid the heated

Do not befriend the heated man,
nor approach him for conversation.
Keep your tongue from answering your superior,
and take care not to insult him.

Let him not cast his speech to lasso You,
Nor give free rein to your answer.
Converse with a man of your own measure,
and take care not to [vex].

Swift is speech when the heart is hurt,
more than wind [over] water.
He tears down, (and) he builds up with his tongue,
when he makes his hurtful speech.
He gives an answer worthy of a beating,
for its weight is harm.
He hauls freight like all the world,
but his load is falsehood.

He is the ferryman of snaring words,
he goes and comes with quarrels.

When he eats and drinks inside,
his answer is (heard) outside.

The day he is charged with his crime,
is misfortune for his children.

If only Khnum came to him !
The potter to the fiery-mouthed man,
so as to knead his [states of mind].
He is like a young wolf in the farmyard,
he turns one eye against the other,
he causes brothers to quarrel,
he runs before every wind like clouds,
he dims the radiance of the Sun,
he flips his tail like the crocodile's young,
[he gathers himself together, crouched.]

His lips are sweet, his tongue is bitter.
A fire burns in his belly.

Do not leap up to join such a one,
lest a terror carry You away.

Chapter 10 : speak without injuring

Do not force yourself to salute the heated man,
for then You injure your own heart.

Do not say "Greetings !" to him falsely,
while there is terror in your belly.

Do not speak falsely to a man,
the god abhors it !

Do not sever your heart from your tongue, (so)
that all your strivings may succeed.
You will be weighty before the others,
and secure in the hand of the god.

God hates the falsifier of words.
He greatly abhors he who quarrels in the belly.

Chapter 11 : abuse no poor

Do not covet a poor man's goods,
nor hunger for his bread.
A poor man's goods are a block in the throat,
it makes the gullet vomit.

He who makes gain by lying oaths,
his heart is misled by his belly.
Where there is fraud, success is feeble, (and)
the bad spoils the good.
You will be guilty before your superior,
and confused in your speech.

Your pleas will be answered by a curse,
your prostrations by a beating.

The big mouthful of bread You swallow,
You vomit it, and You are emptied of your gain.
Observe the overseer of the poor,
when the stick attains him.
All his people are bound in chains,
and he is led to the executioner.

(And) if You are released before your superior,
yet You are hateful to your subordinates.

Steer away from the poor man on the road.
Look at him and keep clear of his goods.

Chapter 12 : always be honest

Do not desire a noble's wealth,
nor give a big mouthful of bread.
If he sets You to manage his property,
shun his, and yours will prosper.

Do not [seize the word] with a heated man,
nor befriend a hostile man.

If You are sent to transport straw,
stay away from its container.
If a man is observed on a fraudulent errand,
he will never (again) be sent on another occasion.

Chapter 13 : write no falsehoods and acquit debt

Do not cheat a man (through) pen on scroll !
The god abhors it !

Do not bear witness with false words,
so as to brush aside a man by your tongue.
Do not assess a man who has nothing,
and thus falsify your pen.

If You find a large debt against a poor man,
make it into three parts,
forgive two, let one stand.
You will find it a path of life.
After sleep, when You wake in the morning,
You will find it as good news !

Better is praise with the love of men,
than wealth in the storehouse.
Better is bread with a happy heart,
than wealth with vexation.

Chapter 14 : be dignified

Do not recall yourself to a man,
nor labour to seek his hand.

If he says to You : "Here is a gift.",
no have-not will refuse it.
Do not blink at him, nor bow your head,
nor turn aside your gaze.
Salute him with your mouth, say : "Greetings !"
He will cease, and You succeed.

Do not rebuff him in his approach, (for)
[on another occasion he will be taken away.]

Chapter 15 : cheat not with your pen

Do the good and You will prosper [as I] !
Do not dip your pen to injure a man, (for)
the finger of the scribe is the beak of the Ibis,
beware of brushing it aside !

The Ape dwells in the House of Khmun,
his eye encircles the Two Lands.
When he sees one who cheats with his finger,
he carries his livelihood off in the flood.

The scribe who cheats with his finger,
his son will not be enrolled.
If You make your life with these (words) in your heart,
your children will observe them.

Chapter 16 : do not corrupt the balance

Do not tamper the scales, nor falsify the weights, nor diminish the fractions of the measure.

Do not desire a measure of the fields, (and then) neglect those of the treasury.

The Ape sits by the balance,
his heart is in the plummet.
Where is a god as great as Thoth ?
Who invented these things and made them ?

Do not make for yourself deficient weights,
they are rich in grief through the might of god.

If You see someone who cheats,
keep your distance from him.
Do not covet copper,
disdain beautiful linen.
What good is one dressed in finery,
if he cheats before the god ?
Faience disguised as gold,
comes morning, (and) it turns to lead.

Chapter 17 : do not corrupt the measure

Beware of disguising the wedjat-measure,
so as to falsify its fractions.
Do not force it to overflow,
nor let its belly be empty.
Measure according to its true size,
your hand clearing exactly.
Do not make a bushel of twice its size,
for then You are headed for the flood.
The bushel is the Eye of Re,
it abhors him who trims.
A measurer who indulges in cheating,
his Eye seals (the verdict) against him.
Do not accept a farmer's dues,
and then assess him so as to injure him.
Do not conspire with the measurer,
so as to defraud the share of the residence.

Greater is the might of the threshing floor,
than an oath by the great throne.

Chapter 18 : be not over-anxious

Do not lie down at night in fear of tomorrow :
"Comes day, how will tomorrow be ?"
Man ignores how tomorrow will be.
The god is ever in his perfection.
The man is ever in his failure.

The words men say are one thing, (but)
the deeds of the god are another.

Do not say : "I have done no wrong.",
and then labour to seek a quarrel.
The wrong belongs to the god.
He seals (the verdict) with his finger.

There is no perfection before the god,
but there is failure before him.
If one labours to seek perfection,
in a moment he has marred it.

Keep firm your mind,
(and) steady your (physical) heart.
do not steer with your tongue.
If a man's tongue is the boat's rudder,
the Lord of All is yet its pilot.

Chapter 19 : do not commit perjury

Do not go to court before an official
in order to falsify your words.
Do not vacillate in your answers,
when your witnesses accuse.
Do not labour (with) oaths by your Lord,
(with) speeches at the hearing.

Tell the truth before the official,
lest he lay a hand on You.

If another day You come before him, he will incline to all
You say, he will relate your speech to the Council of
Thirty, (and) it will be observed on another occasion.

Chapter 20 : be honest as judge or scribe

Do not confound a man in the law court,
in order to brush aside one who is right.
Do not incline to the well-dressed man,
and rebuff the one in rags.

Do not accept the gift of a powerful man,
and deprive the weak for his sake.

Ma'at is a great gift of god.
He gives it to whom he wishes.
(Indeed), the might of him who resembles him,
saves the poor from his tormentor.

Do not make for yourself false documents,
they are a deadly provocation,
they (mean) the great restraining oath,
they (mean) a hearing by the herald.

Do not falsify the oracles in the scrolls,
and thus disturb the plans of god.

Do not use for yourself the might of god,
as if there were no Shay and Renenet.
Hand over property to its owners,
thus do You seek life for yourself.
Do not raise your heart's desire in their house,
or your bones belong to the execution-block.

Chapter 21 : be reticent

Do not say : "Find me a strong superior,
for a man in your town has injured me.'
Do not say : 'Find me a protector,
for one who hates me has injured me."

Indeed You do not know the plans of god,
and should not weep for tomorrow.
Settle in the arms of the god,
your silence will overthrow them.
The crocodile that makes no sound,
dread of it is ancient !

Do not empty your belly to everyone,
and thus destroy respect of You.
Broadcast not your words to others,
nor join with one who bares his heart.

Better is one whose speech is in his belly,
than he who tells it to cause harm.

One does not run to reach perfection,
one does not create (it) to harm it.

Chapter 22 : provoke no enemy

Do not provoke your adversary,
so as to (make) him tell his thoughts.
Do not leap to come before him,
when You do not see his doings.
First gain insight from his answer,
then keep still and You will succeed.
Leave it to him to empty his belly,
know how to sleep, he will be found out.

Grasp his feet, do not harm him.
Be wary of him, do not ignore him.
Indeed, You do not know the plans of god,
and should not weep for tomorrow.
Settle in the arms of the god, (and)
your silence will overthrow them.

Chapter 23 : mind your table manners

Eat no bread in the presence of an official,

and then set your mouth before (him).
If You are sated, pretend to chew,
content yourself with your saliva.

Look at the bowl that is before You,
and let it serve your needs.

An official is great in his office,
as a well is rich in drawings of water.

Chapter 24 : have discretion

Do not listen to an official's reply indoors,
in order to repeat it to another outside.
Do not let your word be carried outside,
Lest your heart be aggrieved.

The heart of man is a gift of god,
beware of neglecting it.
The man at the side of an official, (truly)
his name should not be known.

Chapter 25 : respect god's will

Do not laugh at a blind man.
Nor tease a dwarf.
Nor cause hardship for the lame.
Do not tease a man who is in the hand of the god,
nor be angry with him for his failings.
Man is clay and straw,
the god is his builder.

He tears down, he builds up daily.
He makes a thousand poor by his will.
He makes a thousand men into chiefs,
when he (the god) is in his hour of life.

Happy is he who reaches the West,
when he is safe in the hand of the god.

Chapter 26 : respect seniors

Do not sit down in the beerhouse,
in order to join one greater than You.

Be he a youth great through his office,
or be he an elder through birth.

Befriend a man of your own measure,
Re is helpful from afar.

If You see one greater than You outdoors,
walk behind him respectfully.

Give a hand to an elder sated with beer,
respect him as his children would.

The arm is not hurt by being bared.
The back is not broken by bending it.

A man does not lose by speaking sweetly,
nor does he gain if his speech is straw.

The pilot who sees from afar,
he will not wreck his boat.

Chapter 27 : do not revile an elder

Do not revile one older than You, (for) he has seen Re before You.

Let (him) not report You to the Aten at his rising,
saying : "A youth has reviled an old man."

Very painful before Re,
is a youth who reviles an elder.

Let him beat You while your hand is on your chest, let him revile You while You are silent. If the next day You come before him, he will give You food in plenty.

A dog's food is from its master, (and)
he barks to him who gives it.

Chapter 28 : be generous to the poor

Do not seize a widow when You find her in the fields,
and then fail to be patient with her reply.
Do not refuse your oil jar to a stranger.
Double it before your brothers.
God loves him who honors the poor,
to him who worships the wealthy.

Chapter 29 : travel honestly

Do not prevent people from crossing the river,
if You stride freely in the ferry.

When You are given an oar in the midst of the deep,
bend your arms and take it.
It is no crime in the hand of the god,
[If the sailor does not welcome You.]

Do not make yourself a ferry on the river,
and then labour to seek its fare.

Take the fare from him who is wealthy,
and let pass him who is poor.

Chapter 30 : epilogue

Look to these thirty chapters :
they inform, they educate,
they are the foremost of all books,
they make the ignorant wise.
If they are read to the ignorant,
he is cleansed through them.
Be filled with them, put them in your heart,
and become a man who interprets them,
one who explains as a teacher.

The scribe who is skilled in his office,
is found worthy to be a courtier.'

colophon

That is its end. Written by Senu, son of the divine father Pemu.

Wall relief of the goddess Ma'at
Museo Archeologico Nazionale of Florence

The Adoration of Re

early XIX Dynasty – from the *Papyrus of Ani* – New Kingdom – ca.1250 BCE [13]

Adoration of Re when He rises in the Eastern Horizon of Heaven, by the Osiris scribe of the Holy Offerings, Ani.

He says :

'Homage to You, who are come as Khepri,
Khepri who is the Creator of the Gods.

You rise and shine,
making (all) bright on the back of your Mother (the sky), having appeared in glory as King of the Gods.

With her own hands Mother Nut
performs the pouring of the libation for You.
The mountains of Manu receive You in peace,
(and) Ma'at embraces You at all seasons.

May You give splendour and power in vindication,
-and a coming out as a living soul to see Horus of the Double Horizon- to the Ka of the Osiris scribe Ani,
true of voice before Osiris.'

He says :

'O all You Gods of the House of the Soul,
Weighers of Heaven and Earth in the Balance,
givers of food and sustenance ; (O) Tatenen,
Unique One, Creator of Humanity !
(O) Southern, Northern, Western, and Eastern
Enneads, give praise to Re, Lord of Heaven, the
Sovereign, -Live, Strength, Health-
Creator of the Gods !

Adore Him in his Beautiful Image,
when He ascends in the Bark of the Morning.

May those above worship You,
may those below worship You !
Thoth and Ma'at are your recorders every day !

Your serpent-foe has been given over to the fire and the rebel-serpent is fallen, his arms are bound, Re has taken away his movements, and as for the sons of impotent revolt, they have no being.

The House of the Prince is in Festival,
the voice of those rejoicing is in the Great Place.
The Gods rejoice when they see Re when He ascends,
His rays flood the lands.
The Majesty of this noble God proceeds,
He has entered the land of Manu.
His birth brightens dawn every day ;
He has arrived at His place of yesterday.

May You be satisfied with me.
May I see your beauties !
May I advance upon the Earth !
May I smite the ass !
May I drive off the rebel-serpent !
May I destroy Apep at his moment !
May I see the Abdju-fish at his time of
appearance, and the Inet-fish when it appears,
and the Inet-boat in its pool.

May I see Horus as helmsman,
with Thoth and Ma'at at His two sides.
May I taken hold of the prow of the Bark of Evening,
and the stern of the Bark of Morning.

May He grant me to see the Disk of the Sun, and grant me the sight of the Moon-god unceasingly, every day.

May my soul come forth to walk
to every place it pleases.

May my name be proclaimed when found upon the board of offerings ; may my food offerings be given in my presence like (to) the Followers of Horus.

May a seat be made for me in the Solar bark on the day when the God ferries across.

May I be received in the presence of Osiris in the Land of Vindication.'

To the Ka of Osiris Ani.

Miniature shrine
after an XVIIIth Dynasty model

Notes

Introductions, hieroglyphs, notes, comments and additional bibliography are available at : *www.maat.sofiatopia.org*.

(1) The 'earliest' instruction is the Teaching of Prince Hordedef, son of Khufu, IVth Dynasty, ca. 2571 – 2548. Only a fragment of the text has survived (namely the beginning). It has been pieced together using relatively late copies, namely 9 ostraca of the New Kingdom and one wooden tablet of the Late Period (Brunner-Traut, 1940). The text is archaic enough to be (late) Old Egyptian, i.e. a text supposedly copied without major alterations. Compared with the language of the monumental record, scholars situate its composition in the Vth Dynasty. The tomb of Hardjedef, as he is also known, has been located at Giza, to the east of the pyramid of his father Khufu. Hardjedef also appears later in stories compiled during the Middle Kingdom. A lot of wisdom-teachings are attributed to him, but time has left us nothing but a few ostraca.

www.maat.sofiatopia.org/ptahhotep.htm

(2) The second Old Kingdom instruction is that to Kagemni (serving under Huni and Snefru, IIIth to IVth Dynasty). Of this *Instructions to Kagemni* only the final portion is preserved and the name of the sage is lost. But, the text is part also of *Papyrus Prisse* and (after a blank stretch) it is followed by the *Maxims of Ptahhotep*. Clearly, the fact *Papyrus Prisse* contains both texts makes it the oldest compendium of wisdom teachings extant on papyrus. Although the context of the teaching (to Kagemni) claims to be late IIIth Dynasty, its language is characterized by the schematics of Middle Egyptian encountered in the text of the *Maxims*, which claims to be late Vth Dynasty. As only the wisdom teachings were transmitted in the name of a famous sage (all other literature being anonymous), we may presume this name is indicative of a school of thought initiated by a great historical figure.

www.maat.sofiatopia.org/ptahhotep.htm

(3) Although at present no consensus among scholars exists, I agree with Lichtheim the texts of Kagemni and Ptahhotep are pseudo-epigraphic. This does not exclude the possibility of a line of transmission going back to the author.

In the case of Ptahhotep, this is suggestive of a 'Memphite school' or a community of scribes working in the 'House of Life' of the temple of Ptah at Memphis. Of this only circumstantial evidence and no direct proof exists. The *Maxims* are a pseudo-epigraphic wisdom-text written by an unknown author who, by means of a set of literary devices (such as a pseudo-epigraphic attribution, a compositional context, a narrative structure, a 'count' of good works, etc.), tried to impart the non-polemic, moral philosophy of the Old Kingdom. This author saw in the historical vizier Ptahhotep a recent, grand example of Ma'at everybody still knew, would recognize and might adhere to. These considerations point to the following redactional levels :
• extant text : *Papyrus Prisse*, the oldest papyrus extant, dating XIth Dynasty (ca. 2081 – 1938 BCE) ;
• original text : probably written in early Middle Egyptian in the late VIth Dynasty (ca. 2348 – 2198 BCE) ;
• original ideas : not much later as the period proposed in the extant text ? Djedkare of the late Vth Dynasty, reigned between ca. 2411 and 2378 BCE. The legend of wisdom-teachers goes back to Imhotep, the architect of Djoser of the IIIth Dynasty, ca.2654 – 2635 BCE.

www.maat.sofiatopia.org/ptahhotep.htm

(4) The tomb of Unas was photographed in 1950 by L.F. Husson under Rambova's direction (in Piankoff, A., *The Pyramid of Unas*, 1968). These were scanned, enhanced and combined into a whole at : www.maat.sofiatopia.org/wenis_tomb.htm. A commentary on the text is also available. Take note of better pictures at : www.pyramidtextsonline.com.

www.maat.sofiatopia.org/wenis.htm

(5) The text of the *Instruction to Merikare* was preserved in three fragmentary papyri. The oldest, dating from the second half of the XVIIIth Dynasty (ca. 1539 – 1292 BCE), the so-called *Papyrus St.-Petersburg* (1116A), is the most complete, but also the most corrupt, with numerous lacunae and many scribal errors. *Papyrus Moscow* (4658) dates from the end of the XVIIIth Dynasty, while *Papyrus Carlsberg* (6) may even be later. The following temporal layers may be discerned :
• extant papyri : in the XVIIIth Dynasty, unknown (student ?) scribes made copies from earlier sources - *Papyrus St.-Petersburg* dates from the reign of Pharaoh Amenhotep II (ca. 1426 – 1400 BCE), and was copied in Memphis by 'the scribe Khaemwaset for himself'.

- the actual literary composition : contemporary egyptologists assume the work to be composed in the XIIth Dynasty (ca. 1938 – 1759 BCE). It may be pseudo-epigraphic and composed in the reign of king Merikare. Indeed, the text shows compositional weaknesses, pointing to possible experimentation.
- the person of Merikare : king Merikare ('mrii-kA-ra' - dates unknown), was one of the rulers of the Herakleopolitan IXth Dynasty (ca.2160 – ? BCE). He appears to have been middle-aged when Khety III bequeathed him the throne of the North. He died before the armies of Mentuhotpe II advanced upon his capital. Ity was his successor, but the latter lost the throne.

The salient literary features are :

- the literary form : the orational style is used, a rhythmic style marked by symmetrical sentences, but the text turns into prose when specific events are told (as in the assassination scene in the *Instruction of Amenemhat*).
- the literary aim : the king bestows his insights on kingship in a literary genre : the '*speculum regnum*' - apparently this was not the first instruction of this kind, although the earlier work by the hand of a member of the 'house of Khety' is lost. This *speculum regnum* is in reality a sort of inaugural address of Khety's son Merikare, clothing political intentions with a literary mantle.
- the historical section : the king describes his accomplishments and gives his advise on how to continue them. As far as authorship is concerned, the work is pseudepigraphic, but genuine as a text describing historical facts, probably contemporary with the events to which it refers.
- the definition and workings of magic : the Sun-god Re created magic as a weapon to ward off the blows of evil, a power watching over the good leaders of men day and night. The limits of this power : magic can not hold back the soul of the justified deceased, returning to the place it knows and cares for.
- the section of justice : the justice of the god is all-comprehensive, for he sees all and nobody can resist him. He wants us to do justice, to uphold the correct order (Ma'at). Men are to work for the god, and then the latter will work for them.
- the Hymn to the Sun-god : the Sun-god has created men as his cattle, and he tends it well. He made mankind after his image, and made daylight for their sake. He knows every name and has slain the traitors who made rebellion.

www.maat.sofiatopia.org/merikare.htm

(6) www.maat.sofiatopia.org/heka.htm

(7) This famous work is preserved in a single manuscript from the XIIth Dynasty. In 1843, the egyptologist Lepsius puchased this nameless hieratic papyrus and brought it to Berlin were it became *Berlin Papyrus* 3024. In 1859, he published the text without translation. The first transcription and translation was by Adolf Erman in 1896, under the title : *Das Gespräch eines Lebensmüden mit seiner Seele*. The Egyptian text can also (partly) be found in Sethe's *Aegyptische Lesestücke* (1928). Faulkner published his translation as : 'The Man who was tired of Life'. His work was based on more recent philological insights. In 1969, Wilfrid Barta studied the work. He took 37 translations into account. He stressed the difficulties posed by the text, understood by him as unparalleled among the texts of Ancient Egypt. In 1970, Goedicke published his translation in *The Report about the Dispute of a Man with his Ba*. In 1973, Miriam Lichtheim (who described this text as exceedingly difficult and intriguing) proposed a new translation, but she acknowledged that a great variety of interpretations are possible. In 1978, Bika Reed translated the text from the perspective of the initiatic experience. Another translation in French was done by Claire Lalouette in 1984.

The present translation owes much to the translations of Faulkner, Lichtheim, Reed, Lalouette and made also use of the Egyptian texts published by Faulkner, Sethe and Reed.

www.maat.sofiatopia.org/ba.htm

(8) The text of the *Instruction of Amememhat* was preserved on the so-called *Papyrus Millingen* of the XVIIIth Dynasty, of which an integral copy was made by Peyron in 1843. The papyrus was subsequently lost ! It must have been a good manuscript, turning fragmentary in its final portion. Parts of the work are preserved on three wooden tablets of the XVIIIth Dynasty, papyrus fragments, leather fragments and numerous ostraca of the New Kingdom.

The following temporal layers may be discerned :

• Papyrus Millingen : in the XVIIIth Dynasty, an unknown scribe made a copy from earlier sources. Gardiner (1934), dates the papyrus in the reign of Pharaoh Amenhotep II (ca. 1426 – 1400 BCE) or Tuthmosis IV (ca. 1400 – 1390 BCE).

- the actual composition : the instruction was written shortly after the murder of Amenemhat, namely at the beginning of the reign of king Senusret I, ca. 1909 BCE ;
- the person of Amenemhat : reigned between ca. 1938 – 1909 BCE.

Three literary elements are important :

- the literary form : the orational style is used, except for the description of the assassination, which is in prose ;
- the literary setting : the speaker is the murdered Amenemhat who communicates to his son Senusret in a 'revelation of truth', a device also found in Shakespeare's *Hamlet*.
- the existential tone : as would later be said of the office of the vizier, kingship is not sweet but bitter, and the instruction involves the castigation of the traitors as well as warnings to his son not to trust anybody.

www.maat.sofiatopia.org/amenemhat.htm

(9) Between 1883 and 1884, Urbain Bouriant, thank goodness, made a copy of the *Great Hymn* in the tomb of Aya, a brother of Teye, the mother of Akhenaten (ca. 1353 – 1336 BCE). In 1890, during a quarrel among local inhabitants a third was maliciously destroyed. On the basis of this copy, the famed *Great Hymn to the Aten* could be studied for the first time by James Henry Breasted in 1895 in his Berlin dissertation : *De Hymnis in Solem sub Rege Amenophide IV conceptis.* This text is the basis of what I call 'the Aten-project' of this remarkable king.

www.maat.sofiatopia.org/aten.htm

(10) The series of songs or hymns dedicated to the glorification of Amun are the subject of *Papyrus Leiden* (I 350). This document was probably originally divided in 28 'enclosures' ('Hwt') or 'chapters', of which only 22 have survived in whole or in part (1 through 4 and the last 2 are lost).

www.maat.sofiatopia.org/amun.htm

(11) The *Shabaka Stone* (British Museum 498) is a heavy, nearly black slab of 'Green breccia' from Wadi Hammamat of 137 cm wide. The left side is ca. 91 cm, the right side ca. 95 cm high. With a density of $2.7g/cm^3$, its weight is about 430 kg. It is named after the 'black' Pharaoh Shabaka (ca.712 – 698 BCE),

who ruled in the XXVth Dynasty (ca. 716 – 702 BCE) and who's Old Kingdom styled prenomen ('Neferkare') is mentioned twice (in LINE 1). It was given by the First Lord of the Admiralty George John 2nd Earl Spencer (1758 - 1834) to the British Museum in 1805. It was registered in the inventory of the Museum on the 13th of July of that year. Up to now, its provenance is still unknown. A rectangular squarish hole of 12 cm by 14 cm is cut deep into the stone in the center, out of which eleven rough channels or stripes in length of 25 to 38 cm radiate as a result of ignorant disregard in post-Pharaonic Egypt, when it was probably used as a nether millstone or as a foundation stone. This respectless, rejectable activity has caused a large area of the stone to be worn, with as result the full or partial erasure of 25 lines (LINES 25 - 44) in the center of the inscription, dividing it in two parts : one dealing with Horus' justification to his father's throne (first, left hand side, rendered in a dramatical, responsive way) and the so-called 'theology of Memphis' (last, right hand side, in prose). The scribal voids may refer to the damaged original Pharaoh Shabaka found, namely the outermost edge of a scroll rolled open from left to right. The following redactional levels pertain :

- extant text : ca. 710 BCE (XXVth Dynasty) - end of the Third Intermediate Period.
- original text : ca. 1188 - 1075 BCE (XXth Dynasty) - late New Kingdom. ... lost texts ... other texts ... sapiental literature and *Coffin Texts* of the Middle Kingdom ...
- original idea : 'Sia' and 'Hu' in the *Pyramid Texts* or (late Vth and VIth Dynasties (ca.2378 – 2205).

www.maat.sofiatopia.org/shabaka.htm

(12) The *Instruction of Amen-em-apt*, also called 'Amenemope' or 'Amenophis', son of Kanakht, is one of the numerous treasures which Budge, on his first mission to Egypt, acquired for the (at the time Imperial) British Museum in 1888. Small portions of it were found on a papyrus in Stockholm, three writing tablets in Turin, Paris and Moscow, and an ostracon in the Cairo Museum. This variety points to its popularity. As late as 1923, when the *Budge Papyrus* (BM 10474) was first presented to the public, did the official publication appear in the second series of Budge's famous *Facsimiles of Egyptian Hieratic Papyri in the British Museum*, where the text is photographed, transcribed into hieroglyphs from the original and translated. In his commentary, Sir Wallis drew attention to the resemblance of some passages

to sentences in the *Book of Proverbs* ! Another authoritative translation of the period was that done by Erman (1924). A coherent translation remained far from realized. This was due to the artificial mode of expression, using rare and poetical words and idioms, short phraseology, very few grammatical connectors, short and disconnected sentences, inexact spelling and scribal errors. As the verbal system of Egyptian was refined after the second World War, the philosophy of Amen-em-apt remained long obscure. The following temporal layers pertain :
• the Budge Papyrus : copied by Senu from earlier sources between ca.712 – 332 BCE.
• the actual literary composition : written between ca. 1292 - 1075 BCE.
• the person of Amen-em-apt : lived (or was projected to live) not earlier than ca.1539 BCE.

www.maat.sofiatopia.org/amen_em_apt.htm

(13) The *Papyrus of Ani*, found at Thebes, written in cursive hieroglyphs and illustrated with color vignettes, was purchased by the Trustees of the British Museum run by Sir E.A.Wallis Budge in 1888, where it remains today in the Department of Egyptian Antiquities. The material itself has three layers of papyrus, provided by plants measuring 4.5 inches in the stalks. When unrolled, it became darker and certain sections shrunk. Apparently written by at least three scribes, the vignettes call for fewer artists. The titles of the chapters, rubrics, catch-phrases etc. are in red. At times the text crowds because the artist occupied too much space. The vignettes were probably drawn before the text was written. The different sections of the papyrus were not all originally written for Ani, for in several places his name is entered by a later hand. Such additions do not occur in the first 16 feet and 4 inches. The text has errors, like two copies of a chapter.

For obvious reasons, the original 3200-year-old papyrus cannot be studied. Budge published a corrected hieroglyphic edition without vignettes in 1895 and 1910. A reproduction in a single volume of the original facsimile edition, with hieroglyphic text and vignettes together once more, was done in 1998.

Translations were made by Faulkner, with minor changes added by Goelet (Faulkner died before finishing his work).

The *Papyrus of Ani* is undated and no facts concerning the life of Ani are given. We know he was a scribe, an accountant and an overseer of the granary at Thebes. Ani probably lived during the XIXth Dynasty (ca. 1292 – 1188 BCE), but earlier dates have been suggested (ca. 1450 BCE). But as in the XVIIIth Dynasty, N23 tends to be replaced by N21 (cf. the Gardiner Sign-list), and the latter is found in the text, an early XIXth Dynasty dating seems appropriate.

The original *Papyrus of Ani* measured 78 feet long by 1 foot 3 inches deep. Unfortunately, Budge -in tune with the mentality of the majority of his peers at large- cut the original using the 'yardstick' method, dividing it into thirty-seven sheets of relatively even length, thus disfiguring the flow of the original scroll. Today egyptologists totally reject such practices.

www.maat.sofiatopia.org/adoration_of_re.htm

The hieroglyphs present in this book were created by the author using Inscribe. Likewise with the pictures which were digitally enhanced. The drawings were made using Photoshop. The wooden objects (Seb Ur, Ankh, Shrine) were designed by the author and created at his request by a local artist.

Bibliography

Allen, J.P., *The Inflection of the Verb in the Pyramid Texts*, Undena - Malibu, 1982.
Allen, J.P., *Genesis in Egypt : The Philosophy of Ancient Egyptian Creation Accounts*, Yale Egyptological Seminar - New Haven, 1988.
Allen, J.P., *Religion and Philosophy in Ancient Egypt*, Yale Egyptological Seminar - New Haven, 1989.
Allen, J.P., *Middle Egyptian*, Cambridge University Press - Cambridge, 2000.
Allen, J.P., *The Ancient Egyptian Pyramid Texts*, Society of Biblical Literature - Atlanta, 2005.
Allen, T.G., *Occurrences of Pyramid Texts with Cross-Indexes of these and other Egyptian Mortuary Texts*, University of Chicago Press - Chicago, 1950.
Altenmüller, H., *Die Texts zum Begräbnisritual in den Pyramiden des Alten Reiches*, Wiesbaden, 1972.
Assmann, J., *Ägyptische Hymnen und Gebete*, Artemis - Zurich, 1975.
Assmann, J., *Zeit und Ewigheit im alten Ägypten*, Carl Winter Universitätsverlag - Heidelberg, 1975.
Assmann, J., *The Search for God in Ancient Egypt*, Cornell University Press - London, 1991.
Assmann, J., *Egyptian Solar Religion in the New Kingdom*, Kegan Paul - New York, 1995.
Assmann, J., *Moses the Egyptian*, Harvard University Press - London, 1999.
Assmann, J., *Maât*, La Maison de Vie - Paris, 1999.
Assmann, J., *Images et Rites de la Mort*, Cybele - Paris, 2000.
Assmann, J., *The Mind of Egypt*, Holt - New York, 2002.
Barta, W. : *Die Bedeutung des Pyramidetexts für den verstorben König*, Deutscher Kunstverlag - Berlin, 1981.
Barucq, A. & Daumas, F. *: Hymnes et Prières de L'Égypte Ancienne*, Du Cerf - Paris, 1980.
Bonnet, H., *Reallexicon der ägyptischen Religionsgeschichte*, de Gruyter - Berlin, 1952.
Borghouts, J., *The Magical Texts of Papyrus Leiden*, Brill - Leiden, 1971.
Borghouts, J., *Ancient Magical Texts*, Bril - Leiden, 1978.
Bourguet, De, P., *Grammaire Egyptienne*, Peeters - Leuven, 1980.
Braguet, P., *Les textes des sarcophages égyptiens du Moyen Empire*, du Cerf - Paris, 1986.
Breasted, J.H., *De Hymnis in Solem sub Rege Amenophide IV*

conceptis , Berlin University - dissertation, 1895.
Breasted, J.H., *Development of Religion and Thought in Ancient Egypt*, Pennsylvania University Press - Pennsylvania, 1972.
Breasted, J.H., *Ancient Records of Egypt*, vol.1-5, University of Illinois Press - Illinois, 2001.
Brunner, H., *Die Weisheitsbücher der Ägypter*, Artemis - Zürich, 1991.
Buck, de A., *The Egyptian Coffin Texts*, 7 volumes, Oriental Institute Publications - Chicago, 34, 49, 64, 67, 73, 81, 87, 1935-1961.
Buck, de A., *De Egyptische voorstellingen van den Oerheuvel*, Brill - Leiden, 1922.
Buck, de A., *Egyptian Readingbook*, Nederlandsch Archaeologisch - Philologische Instituut - Leiden, 1948.
Budge, E.A.W., *Facsimiles of Eyptian hieratic Papyri*, London, 1910.
Budge, E.A.W., *The Book of the Dead*, Dover - New York, 1967.
Budge, E.A.W. : *An Egyptian Hieroglyphic Dictionary*, 2 volumes, Dover - New York, 1978.
Budge, E.A.W., *A Hieroglyphic Vocabulary of the Book of the Dead*, Dover - New York, 1991.
Budge, E.A.W., *An Introduction to Ancient Egyptian Literature*, Dover - New York, 1997.
Carrier, Cl., *Textes des Sarcophages du Moyen Égyptien*, Du Rocher - Paris, 2004, 3 volumes.
Davies, N. de G., *The Mastaba of Ptahhetep and Akhethetep at Saqqareh*, part I, The Egypt Exploration Fund - London, 1900.
Davies, N. de G., *The Rock Tombs of El Amarna*, The Egypt Exploration Fund - London, 1905/1908.
Davies, W.V., *Reading the Past : Egyptian Hieroglyphs*, British Museum Press - London, 1995.
Dévaud, E., *Les Maximes de Ptahhotep d'après le papyrus Prisse, les Papyrus 10371 et 1059 du British Museum et la Tablette Carnarvon*, Fribourg, 1916.
Erman, A. & Grapow, H., *Wörtenbuch der ägyptischen Sprache im Auftrage der deutschen Akademien*, Akademie Verlag - Berlin, 1957-63.
Erman, A., *The Ancient Egyptians : a sourcebook of their Writings*, New York, (1927) 1966.
Erman, A., *Die Religion der Ägypter*, Berlin, 1934.
Faulkner, R.O., *The Ancient Egyptian Pyramid Texts*, Oxford University Press - Oxford, 1969.
Faulkner, R.O., *The Ancient Egyptian Coffin Texts*, 3 volumes, Aris & Phillips - Warminster, 1973.
Faulkner, R.O., *A Concise Dictionary of Middle Egyptian*, Griffith Institute - Oxford, 1999.

Faulkner, R.O., *The Egyptian Book of the Dead*, Chronicle Books - San Francisco, 1998.
Gardiner, A., *Late Egyptian Stories*, La Fondation Égyptologique Reine Elisabeth - Brussels, 1932.
Gardiner, A., *The earliest Manuscripts of the Instruction of Amenemmes I*, in : Maspero, G. : *Mélanges Maspero I*, Le Caire, 1934.
Gardiner, A., *Ancient Egyptian Onomastica*, 2 volumes, Oxford University Press - Oxford, 1947.
Gardiner, A., *The Theory of Speech and_Language*, Clarendon Press - Oxford, 1951.
Gardiner, A., *Egypt of the Pharaohs*, Oxford University Press - Oxford, 1964.
Gardiner, A., *Egyptian Grammar*, Griffith Institute - Oxford, 1982.
Glanville, S.R.K., *The Instructions of 'Onchshesonqy*, Catalogue of Demotic Papyri of the British Museum - London, vol.11, 1955 (BMP 10508).
Goedicke, H., *The Report about the Dispute of a Man with His Ba*, Baltimore, 1970.
Goelet, O., *The Egyptian Book of the Dead*, Chronicle Books - San Francisco, 1998.
Harrington, N., Living with the Dead, Oxbow Books – Oxford, 2013.
Helck, W., *Der Text der 'Lehre Amenemhets I für seinen Sohn'*, Harrassowitz - Wiesbaden, 1969.
Helck, W., *Die Lehre für König Merikare*, KÄT - Wiesbaden, 1977.
Jacq, Ch., *La Sagesse Égyptienne*, Du Rocher - Paris, 1981.
Jacq, Ch., *L'Enseignement du sage Égyptien Ptahhotep*, La Maison de Vie - Paris, 1993.
Jéquier, G., *Le papyrus Prisse et ses variantes*, Paris, 1911.
Kemp, B., The City of Akhenaten and Nefertiti, Thames & Hudson – London, 2015.
Lange, H.O., *Das Weisheitsbuch des Amenemope*, Host - Copenhagen, 1925.
Lange, H.O., *Der magische Papyrus Harris*, Host - Copenhagen, 1927.
Lalouette, Cl., *Textes Sacrés et Textes Profanes de l'Ancienne Egypte I & II*, Gallimard - Paris, 1984, 1987.
Loprieno, A., *Ancient Egytian : A Linguistic Introduction*, Cambridge University Press - Cambridge, 1995.
Maspero, G., *Les enseignements d'Amenemhat Ier à son fils Sanouastris Ier*, Cairo, 1914.
Mercer, S.A.B., *The Pyramid Texts*, 3 volumes, Longmans, Green and C° - London, 1952.

Mercer, S.A.B., *Literary Criticism of the Pyramid Texts*, Luzac & C° - London, 1956.
O'Connor, D., Abydos, Thames & Hudson – London, 2011.
Parkinson, R., *The Tale of Sinuhe and Other Ancient Egyptian Poems*, Oxford University Press - Oxford, 1997.
Piaget, J., *Biologie et Connaissance*, Collection Idées – Paris 1967,
Piaget, J., *The development of thought. Equilibration of cognitive structures*, Oxford University Press –Oxford 1978.
Piankoff, A., *Le 'coeur' dans les textes égyptiennes*, PUF - Paris, 1930.
Piankoff, A., *The Pyramid of Unas*, Princeton University Press - Princeton, 1968.
Piankoff, A., *Wanderings of the Soul*, Princeton University Press - Princeton, 1974.
Rankine, D., *Heka*, Avalonia - England, 2006.
Rocati, A., *La Littérature Historique sous l'Ancient Empire Egyptien*, du Cerf - Paris, 1982.
Rothöhler, B., *Neue Gedanken zum Denkmal memphitischer Theologie*, Heidelberg, 2004.
Sethe, K., *Die Altägyptischen Pyramidentexte*, 4 volumes, Darmstadt - Wissenschaftliche Buchgesellschaft, 1908/1960.
Sethe, K., *Übersetzung und Kommentar zu den altägyptischen Pyramidentexten*, 6 volumes, Augustin - Hamburg, 1935-1962.
Sethe, K., *Ägyptische Lesestücke*, Olms - Hildesheim, 2001.
Wasserman, J., *The Egyptian Book of the Dead*, Cronicle Books - San Francisco, 1998.
Shepherd, R.D., *Grace Abounding*, Core Knowledge Foundation – Charlottesville, 2006.
Zába, Z., *Les Maximes de Ptahhotep*, Éditions de l'Academie Tchécoslovatique des Sciences - Prague, 1956.
Zabkar, L., *A Study of the Ba Concept in Ancient Egyptien Texts*, Studies in Ancient Oriental Civilization - Chicago, 34, 1968.

Abou Ghazi, D., 'Bewailing the King in the Pyramid Texts.', in : Bulletin de l'Institut Français d'Archéologie Orientale du Caire - Cairo, n°66, 1968, pp.157-164.
Abou Ghazi, D., 'The First Appearance of Re and His Continuous Being as Depicted in the Pyramid Texts.', in : Ibidem, n°68, 1969, pp.47-51.
Allen, J.P., 'Reading a Pyramid.', in : Hommages Leclant, I, 1988, pp.5-28.
Altenmüller, H., 'Denkmal memphitischer Theologie.' in : Lexicon der Ägyptologie, 1:1065-1069.
Altenmüller, H., 'Bemerkungen zum Kannibalenspruch.' in :

Assmann, J., Feucht, E. & Grieshammer, R., *Fragen an die altägyptische Literatur*, Reichert - Wiesbaden, 1977, pp.19-39.
Assmann, J., 'Akhanyati's Theology of Light and Time.', in : Proceedings of the Israel Academy of Sciences and Humanities - Jeruzalem, 7, n°4, 1992, pp.143-175.
Assmann, J., 'When Justice Fails.', in : Journal of Egyptian Archeology - London, 1992, pp.149-162.
Assmann, J., 'Semiosis and Interpretation in Ancient Egyptian Ritual.', in : Bidermann & Scharfstein : Interpretation in Religion, Brill - Leiden, 1992, pp.87-109.
Assmann, J., 'Ancient Egypt and the Materiality of the Sign.', in : Gumbrechts, H.U. & Pfeiffer, K.L. (editors) : *Materialities of Communication*, Stanford University Press - California, 1994.
Barguet, P., 'Les chapitres 313-321 des Textes des Pyramides et la naissance de la lumière.', in Revue d'Égyptologie, 22, 1970, pp.7-14.
Barta, W., 'Untersuchungen zur Göttlichkeit des regierenden Königs.', in : Münchner Ägyptologische Studien, 32, Berlin, 1975.
Barta, W., 'Zu den Schilfbündelsprüchen der Pyramidetexte.' in : Studien zur Altägyptischen Kultur, 2, 1975, pp.39-48.
Barta, W., 'Das Gespräch eines Mannes mit seinem Ba.', in : Münchner ägyptologische Studien, Hessling, Berlin, n°18, 1969.
Brunner-Traut, E., 'The Instruction of Hardjedef.', in Zeitschrift für ägyptische Sprache und Altertumskunde, 76, 1940, pp.3-9 and plate 1.
Cazemier, L.J., 'Das Gebet in der Pyramidentexten.', in : Jaarbericht van het Vooraziatisch - Egyptisch Genootschap 'Ex Oriente Lux', 15, 1957-1958, pp.47-65.
Chabas, F., 'Le plus ancien livre du monde. Etude sur le Papyrus Prisse.', in : Revue archéologique, XXV, 1858, pp.1-25.
Erman, A., 'Die ägyptischen Beschwörungen des grossen Pariser Zauberpapyrus.', in : Zeitschrift für ägyptische Sprache und Altertumskunde, 21, 1883, pp.89-109.
Erman, A., 'Gespräch eines Lebensmüden mit seiner Seele.', in : Abhandlungen der Preussischen Akademie der Wissenschaften - Berlin, 1896.
Erman, A., 'Ein Denkmal memphitischer Theologie.', in : Sitzungsberichte der Preussischen Akademie der Wissenschaften - Berlin, 43, 1911.
Erman, A., 'Der Leidener Amonshymnus.', in : Ibidem, 1923.
Faulkner, R.O., 'The man who was tired of life.', in : Journal for Egyptian Archeaology, 42, 1956, pp.21-40.
Faulkner, R.O., 'The King and the Star-Religion in the Pyramid Texts.", in : Journal of Near Eastern Studies, 25, 1966, pp.153-161.

Foster, J.L., 'Some Observations on Pyramid Texts 273-274 : the so-called "Cannibal Hymn".', in : Journal of the Society for the Study of Egyptian Antiquities, 9, 1978-1979, pp.51-63.
Gardiner, A., 'The Instruction to Merikare.', in : Journal of Egyptian Archaeology - London, 1914, pp.20-36.
Gardiner, A., 'The Eloquent Peasant.', in : Journal of Egyptian Archaeology - London, 9, 1923, pp.5-25.
Gardiner, A., 'The House of Life.', in : Journal of Egyptian Archaeology - London, 24, 1938, pp.157-179.
Gardiner, A., 'The Mansion of Life and the Master of the King's Largess.', in : Journal of Egyptian Archaeology - London, 24, 1938, pp.83-91.
Gardiner, A., 'The Instruction to Kagemni and his brethren.', in : Journal of Egyptian Archaeology - London, 32, 1946, pp.71-74.
Gardiner, A., 'Kagemni once again.', in : Journal of Egyptian Archaeology - London, 37, 1951, brief communications, pp.109-110.
Griffith, F.L., 'The Millingen Papyrus.', in : Zeitschrift fur ägyptologische Sprache und Altertumskunde, n°34, 1896, pp.35-51.
Griffith, F.L., 'The teachings of Amenophis, the son of Kanakht. - Papyrus BM 10474.', in : Journal of Egyptian Archaeology - London, 12, 1926, pp.191-231.
Junge, F., 'Zur Fehldatierung des Sog.Denkmals memphitischer Theologie oder der Beitrag der ägyptischen Theologie zur Geistesgeschichte der Spätzeit.', in : MItteilungen des Deutschen archäologischen Instituts, Abteilung Kairo, Zabern - Mainz, 1973.
Junker, H., 'Die Götterlehre von Memphis (Shabaka-Inschrift).', in : Abhandlungen der Preussischen Akademie der Wissenschaften, Philosophisch-historische Klasse, Verlag der Akademie der Wissenschaften - Berlin, 1939.
Kraus, R., 'Wie jung ist die memphitische Philosophie auf dem Shabaqo-Stein?' in : 'Gold of Praise : Studies on Ancient Egypt in Honor of Edward F. Wente', in : John A Larson, J.A., Teeter, E. & Wente, E.F., Studies in Ancient Oriental Civilization, n°58, Chicago, Oriental Institute, 1999, pp.239-246.
Leclant, J., 'Shabaka.', in : Lexicon der Ägyptologie, 5:499-513.
Lopez, J., 'Le Papyrus Millingen.', in : Revue d'Égyptologie, 15, 1963, pp.29-33 (pls.4-8).
Osing, J., 'Zur Disposition der Pyramidtexts des Unas.', in : Mitteilungen des Deutschen archäologischen Instituts, abteilung Kairo, 42, 1986, pp.131-144.
Ridley, R.T., 'The Discovery of the Pyramid Texts.', in : Zeitschrift für Ägyptische Sprache und Altertumskunde, 110,

1983, pp.74-80.
Scharff, A., `Die Lehre für Kagemni.', in : Zeitschrift für Ägyptische Sprache und Altertumskunde, 175, 1939, pp.13-21.
Sethe, K., `Das 'Denkmal memphitischer Theologie, der Schabakostein des Britischen Museums.', in : Untersuchungen zur Geschichte und Altertumskunde Ägyptens, Leipzig, 1928, 10, 1.
Sethe, K., `Dramatische Texte zu altaegyptischen Mysterienspielen.', in : Ibidem - Leipzig, 10, 1928.
Sethe, K., `Amun und die acht Urgötter von Hermopolis.', in : Abhandlungen der Preussischen Akademie der Wissenschaften - Berlin, 4, 1929.
Silverman, D.P. : `Textual Criticism in the Coffin Texts.', in Allen, J.P., `Religion and Philosophy in Ancient Egypt.', Yale Egyptological Seminar - New Haven, 1989, pp.29-44.
Simpson, D.C., `The Hebrew Book of Proverbs and the Teaching of Amenophis.', in : Journal of Egyptian Archeology, 12, 1926, pp.232-239.
Stricker, B.H., `De egyptische mysteriën : Papyrus Leiden T 32.', Oudheidkundige Mededelingen uit het Rijksmuseum van Oudheden te Leiden - Leiden, 1950 & 1953.
Tobin, V.A., `Divine Conflict in the Pyramid Texts.', in : Journal of the American Research Center in Egypt - Boston, 30, 1993, pp.93-110.
Wilson, J.A., `The Memphite Theology of Creation.' in : Pritchard, J.B., `The Ancient Near East : An Anthology of Text and Pictures.', Princeton University Press - Princeton, 1958, pp.1-2.
Zabkar, L.V., `A Study of the Ba concept in Ancient Egyptian texts.', in : Studies in Ancient Oriental Civilization, Chicago University Press - Chicago, n°34, 1968.